RT Essentials

Other resources from O'Reilly

Related titles

Essential Business Process Modeling

Essential System Administration

Essential System Administration Pocket Reference

Linux Network Administrator's Guide

Linux Server Security

Managing Security with Snort & IDS Tools

Network Security Assessment

Perl for System Administration

Practical Development Environments

The Art of Project Management

Windows 2000 Administration in a Nutshell

oreilly.com

oreilly.com is more than a complete catalog of O'Reilly books. You'll also find links to news, events, articles, weblogs, sample chapters, and code examples.

oreillynet.com is the essential portal for developers interested in open and emerging technologies, including new platforms, programming languages, and operating systems.

Conferences

O'Reilly brings diverse innovators together to nurture the ideas that spark revolutionary industries. We specialize in documenting the latest tools and systems, translating the innovator's knowledge into useful skills for those in the trenches. Visit *conferences.oreilly.com* for our upcoming events.

Safari Bookshelf (*safari.oreilly.com*) is the premier online reference library for programmers and IT professionals. Conduct searches across more than 1,000 books. Subscribers can zero in on answers to time-critical questions in a matter of seconds. Read the books on your Bookshelf from cover to cover or simply flip to the page you need. Try it today with a free trial.

RT Essentials

Jesse Vincent, Robert Spier, Dave Rolsky,
Darren Chamberlain, and Richard Foley

O'REILLY®

Beijing · Cambridge · Farnham · Köln · Paris · Sebastopol · Taipei · Tokyo

RT Essentials

by Jesse Vincent, Robert Spier, Dave Rolsky, Darren Chamberlain, and Richard Foley

Published by O'Reilly Media, Inc., 1005 Gravenstein Highway North, Sebastopol, CA 95472.

O'Reilly books may be purchased for educational, business, or sales promotional use. Online editions are also available for most titles (*safari.oreilly.com*). For more information, contact our corporate/institutional sales department: (800) 998-9938 or *corporate@oreilly.com*.

Editors:	Allison Randal and Tatiana Apandi
Production Editor:	Darren Kelly
Cover Designer:	Ellie Volckhausen
Interior Designer:	David Futato
Production Services:	Amy Hassos

Printing History:

August 2005:	First Edition.

 This book uses RepKover™, a durable and flexible lay-flat binding.

ISBN: 0-596-00668-3
[M]

Table of Contents

Preface

I first wrote RT because I had to. I was a summer intern for a now-defunct web design shop called Utopia Inc. Half my time was to be spent hacking Perl code for customer projects. The other half of my time, I was to be the office's second sysadmin. The company did most everything by email, including ask the other sysadmin, my boss, to take care of work. Everything the company's 30-member staff needed us to do ended up in her inbox. When I got there, I suggested that we deploy a ticketing system, such as the one I'd set up for my university helpdesk. She seemed to think this was a pretty good idea except she thought we'd be better off if I implemented a new ticketing system from scratch.

At the end of the summer, I managed to convince the company's founders that they should let me take my creation with me, continue to hack on it, and give it away.* Flash forward a couple years: I placed an order for a DSL line with a national DSL provider and got back a ticket from their RT instance. A quick calculation showed that they were creating over 1,000 tickets a day—a couple orders of magnitude more than I'd ever imagined anyone handling with RT. This was just the nudge I needed to rebuild RT from the ground up.

Over the next few years, I found more and more organizations picking RT up for tracking everything from security incidents to sales inquiries to email counseling sessions for troubled teens. Our current best guess is that over 10,000 organizations use RT. The community that has grown up around RT is amazingly vibrant. When you're working with RT either as an administrator or developer, it's quite worthwhile to join the community on *rt-users* and *rt-devel* mailing lists as well as our wiki, *wiki.bestpractical.com*. (We'll talk a bit more about the community in Chapter 10.)

When I first wrote RT in 1996, I had no idea it was going to be more than a summer project. It's been an amazing first nine years.

—Jesse Vincent

---

* It wasn't exactly a hard sell. They thought this was a great idea.

Audience

We designed this book to be useful to end-users, systems administrators, and developers who interact with RT on an occasional or regular basis.

If you're an end user

Start off with Chapter 1 to learn about ticketing systems. Then skip forward to Chapter 3 to find out how to use RT's web interface. If you're comfortable getting things done with command-line interfaces, read Chapter 4 to see how to use and automate RT with *rt*. After that, pick and choose whatever sounds interesting.

If you're a systems administrator

Chapter 1 will give you a background in ticketing systems. Chapter 2 helps you get set up with a live RT instance. After that, jump ahead to Chapter 5 for help setting up users, groups, queues, and access control. Chapter 7 is filled with suggestions for potential uses of RT inside your organization. Once you have RT up and running, chapters 3 and 4 will help with day to day interaction and should make a good guide to help your users get comfortable working with RT on their own.

Once RT is up and running, you should check out the rest of the book, which focuses on development and customization.

If you're a developer

If you're a developer, it probably makes the most sense to read this book straight through before you start hacking. The first section focuses on getting a system up and running. The second section talks about basic customization and configuration. The third section focuses on how RT's code and database are put together.

If you're chomping at the bit to get started, read Chapter 2 to find out the basics of installation, then Chapter 10 to learn a few tricks that will make your development process much smoother. Chapters 9 and 10 will explain how everything fits together.

Assumptions This Book Makes

Except for Chapter 1, this book assumes that you use (or want to use) RT to manage tasks. * As you delve deeper into the book, various sections will be considerably more useful to you if you have at least a basic understanding of the Unix command line, basic Unix systems administration skills, and at least a little bit of experience programming in Perl.

---

* Chapter 1's job is to convince you that you need a system like RT.

What's Inside

Chapter 1, *What Is Ticketing?*
> Provides some background about what ticketing systems are and how they can help save your job and your sanity.

Chapter 2, *Installation*
> Walks you through the process of setting up an RT server and configuring sane system defaults.

Chapter 3, *Getting Started*
> Will help you get up and running with RT's web interface.

Chapter 4, *Command-Line Interface*
> Explains how to interact with RT from your shell or console window.

Chapter 5, *Administrative Tasks*
> Steps you through the basics of turning a virgin RT server into a useful tool for tracking what you need to do inside your organization.

Chapter 6, *Scrips*
> Shows you how to extend RT's standard behavior with custom business logic.*

Chapter 7, *Example Configurations*
> Provides a look inside the RT configuration at Yoyodyne Propulsion Systems, a nonexistent company that makes heavy use of RT to manage their internal processes.

Chapter 8, *Architecture*
> Covers the nuts and bolts of how RT is put together. This chapter walks you through RT's files on disk, as well as the details of its database tables.

Chapter 9, *API*
> Describes how `DBIx::SearchBuilder` works. SearchBuilder is the object-relational mapping framework that ties RT to the database backend.

Chapter 10, *Development Environments*
> Helps you set up a local sandbox for modifying and extending RT without putting your production server in harm's way.

Conventions

Constant width
> Used for literal text, module names, function names, method names, and keywords

Constant width italic
> Used to show text that should be replaced with user-supplied values

---

* Please forgive us for the name *Scrip*. Jesse coined it in the middle of the dot com boom to describe a cross between "script" and "subscription." Everybody was inventing words back then and it seemed like a good idea at the time.

Constant width bold

    Used to show commands or other text that should be typed literally by the user

Italic

    Used for filenames, components, commands, URLs, emphasis, and terms when they are first introduced

Using Code Examples

This book is here to help you get your job done. In general, you may use the code in this book in your programs and documentation. You do not need to contact us for permission unless you're reproducing a significant portion of the code. For example, writing a program that uses several chunks of code from this book does not require permission. Selling or distributing a CD-ROM of examples from O'Reilly books does require permission. Answering a question by citing this book and quoting example code does not require permission. Incorporating a significant amount of example code from this book into your product's documentation does require permission.

We appreciate, but do not require, attribution. An attribution usually includes the title, author, publisher, and ISBN. For example: "RT Essentials by Jesse Vincent, Robert Spier, Dave Rolsky, Darren Chamberlain, and Richard Foley. Copyright 2005 O'Reilly Media, Inc., 0-596-00668-3." If you feel your use of code examples falls outside fair use or the permission given above, feel free to contact us at *permissions@oreilly.com*.

We'd Like to Hear from You

Please send comments and questions concerning this book to the publisher at the following address:

    O'Reilly Media, Inc.
    1005 Gravenstein Highway North
    Sebastopol, CA 95472
    (800) 998-9938 (in the United States or Canada)
    (707) 829-0515 (international or local)
    (707) 829-0104 (fax)

We have a web page for this book, where we list errata, examples, or any additional information. You can access this page at:

    http://www.oreilly.com/catalog/rtessentials

To comment or ask technical questions about this book, send email to:

    bookquestions@oreilly.com

For more information about our books, conferences, Resource Centers, and the O'Reilly Network, see our web site at:

http://www.oreilly.com

Safari® Enabled

 When you see a Safari® enabled icon on the cover of your favorite technology book, that means the book is available online through the O'Reilly Network Safari Bookshelf.

Safari offers a solution that's better than e-Books. It's a virtual library that lets you easily search thousands of top tech books, cut and paste code samples, download chapters, and find quick answers when you need the most accurate, current information. Try it free at *http://safari.oreilly.com*.

Acknowledgments

Neither this book nor RT would be here without the community that has grown around RT since it was first released almost 10 years ago. The thousands of members of the *rt-users* and *rt-devel* mailing-lists have made RT a pleasure to work on and to use.

Nat Torkington is responsible for making this book happen in the first place. Simon Cozens singlehandedly convinced the publisher that an RT book should happen. Our editor, Allison Randal, moved heaven and earth to get the project back on track after what seemed like certain doom.

Last, but only because they all managed to do a fantastic job reviewing this book's content on a very tight schedule at the last minute, we would like to thank our technical reviewers: Todd Chapman, Simon Cozens, Andy Harrison, Phil Homewood, Autrijus Tang, Greg Williamson, and Ruslan Zakirov.

Ruslan is also responsible for the majority of the content on *wiki.bestpractical.com*, which is an incredibly valuable companion to this book.

What Is Ticketing?

If your organization is anything like any of ours, there's always a lot of stuff to do. Vendors need to get paid. Customers need to get invoiced. Staff need to do work for customers. Sales inquiries need to be answered. Bugs in hard- or software need to be fixed, and everyone needs to know that they have been fixed. *Somebody* needs to take out the garbage. And at the end of the day, you've got to know who wanted what, who did it, when it got done, and most importantly what remains *undone*.

That's where a ticketing system comes in.

Why "Ticket"?

The convention is to call each request or piece of work a *Ticket*. When a new thing comes into the system, we give it a virtual slip of paper with a number, much like the ticket for checking your coat at the coat room or leaving your car in valet parking. This is the ticket we track.

A Dissected Ticketing System

Before we get into typical applications, let's dissect a generic ticketing system into its component parts, by building a list of the things a typical ticketing system will do. You can use this list to decide whether or not you need a ticketing system.

These are the bones of a true ticketing system:

- Register an event or a ticket
- Assign an owner, or person responsible, to the ticket
- Assign additional interested parties to the ticket
- Track changes to the ticket
- Inform interested parties of these changes
- Launch activity based on ticket status and/or priority

- Report on status of one or more ticket(s)—an overview
- Finish with, or close, the ticket

Deletions

Note the list doesn't include a "Delete this Ticket" mechanism, even when it is finished, or closed. This is because it is essential for any professional ticketing solution to show the status of a Thing once it's entered into the system and the entire history of how it is handled. You should be able to close a Thing, but not remove knowledge of it, or what happened to it, from the system. On the other hand, it is possible and sometimes even desirable to remove erroneous entries from the system—such as duplicates or plain wrong entries. Deletion may be primarily a manual process, so that people will use it rarely. The prime intention here is to maintain a history of events and the current status, and never to lose it.

While your to do list, sticky notes on the refrigerator, or PDA may be a great *personal* ticketing system for simple lists of things to do, these tools are mediocre at best as a ticketing system for larger projects. Taking a numbered ticket at the supermarket before you can buy meat and cheese at the deli counter is another instance of a short-term but effective system. The same applies to the systems installed at railway stations and doctors' offices.

The concern here is not the short-term view, but the fully-functional system leveraging the power of a database to identify a Thing and follow the course of this Thing through a distinct process to an expected conclusion.

Uses for a Ticketing System

Although ticketing systems come in several flavors, most are designed for a single application. Typical applications, and some of the ways in which a ticketing system can explicitly help, are explained next.

Production Operations Support

Running operations support in a production environment can be very confusing. For example, if a bank financial trading system goes down, the online replacement (hotswap) system needs to step in and take over. Even if this works smoothly, there will be lots of people running around screaming like headless chickens. Under these circumstances it is very easy to see how a fix to a less critical application could be missed or delayed.

You can use a ticketing system to assign tasks as they come in to the next available operative. Tasks which have a higher priority or are critical in nature get fixed first. Simply fixing the current emergency is not enough, though. There needs to be a system in place which tracks the outstanding tasks—the ones temporarily on the back-burner—and identifies which are the most important to solve next. This is what the banks do and for good reason—they work in a permanent state of paranoia. The need for a priority list like this is not limited to banks. It applies to whatever is critical in your environment.

Sales Lead Tracking

A representative of the company is informed of a potential sales lead. This information might come in many forms: a note, an email, a telephone call request, person who hears of a requirement that needs fulfilling, a personal recommendation. What form the lead takes doesn't really matter. The important thing is to not miss the opportunity to *close the sale*.

If you have a sales lead tracking system in place, you can see which leads are still open and need more work. You also can see which salesperson brings in the most leads, and perhaps most important, which salesperson successfully closes the most leads. This information is immediately available at all times via a number of configurable report options.

Without having this information handy, it is very easy to lose promising leads, or to leave half-finished responses unfinished, neither of which improves customer confidence. If a buyer is unable to buy from you, they will buy from someone else.

Customer Service

A customer contacts the company with a query. In this case we are not talking about a purchase but a service request. The request should still be tracked, even if the contact person can immediately solve the query.

Tracking the request ensures the company has a record of what types of queries are most common. This also can give the company instant feedback on whether or not their users find the published documentation or processes hard to understand, merely sufficient, or easy to follow.

Project Management

A ticketing system can track the items in a project management plan. You can see who is responsible for a task and, when he has finished the task, you will know about it when the status changes. In a project management plan, it is critical to have an overview of the dependencies between separate tasks or work flows.

Imagine that you are in charge of developing a new space station or vehicle. You are particularly interested are particularly interested in the exciting new space telescope which will allow astronomers to peer into the beginning of time. It might be easy to miss the importance of an incidental task, such as installing a reliable, bombproof, redundant air supply for the personnel. The safety team, in this case the *interested party*, needs to know that the oxygen supply team, the owner of the task, has completed and tested the installation of the air supplies and backups.

This example may seem obvious, but smaller things have caused immense failures. We only have to remember the tragic Challenger Space Shuttle disaster, where the extremely small O-ring seal failed in part because of the extreme temperatures and in part because of bad management pressure and decisions. You can't ignore essential information or equipment—no matter how small it is.

A complicated and redundant project like the space shuttle has so many checks and counter-checks that a ticketing system might seem irrelevant—yet it needs some way to track all the outstanding tasks and who should work on them.

Network Security

If a system is compromised by a security breach, this event can be entered and tracked as a ticket, and an alert can be sent to the appropriate parties. People responsible for the hardware, the software, the administration, the firewall, the proxy, or the Internet access can be assigned as interested parties to the ticket.

If the documentation team continually gets alerts from network attacks, or if the sales team receives endless notes regarding the current status of a particular firewall configuration, they will start filtering incoming notifications to */dev/null* or the dustbin. Being able to assign the appropriate people from different interest groups to a particular ticket is critical to the smooth running of an efficient ticketing system.

Everyone who needs to know can follow the status of the new security breach: what can be done to fix it, what has been done, and whether the problem has been succesfully fixed and the hole plugged. If you don't track this information, there is a high probability that the same attack will break through your defenses again after you've forgotten when and how the original attack broke through.

Engineering (Bug Tracking)

Many open source projects have a public bugs database where users can check if a problem they have is related to a known bug. The database is essential for tracking the history of bugs over time, for example, to determine if developers already tried a proposed change and rejected it for a valid reason. People can find out if the bug they are trying to report has already been reported and not flood the database with duplicate bug reports.

Bug tracking software has been around a long time. The success or failure of any bug tracking solution often depends on how people use the system. It is not enough to simply enter bugs in a database or tracking tool, and then to fix the bugs. The next step—an essential one—is to close the ticket. Often the QA (Quality Assurance) department will ensure this takes place. A good ticketing system makes this task simple by letting you view the status of all known tickets at once.

The preceding list of potential uses is not exhaustive, but it should give you an idea of the breadth of applications a ticket tracking tool has.

Features of a Ticketing System

We covered the essential bones of a ticketing system, now we'll look at some of the features that make up a succesful solution. All ticketing systems should have the following qualities:

Accessibility
> A ticketing system should be simple to access from wherever you are going to access it. Programmers and programs will want a CLI (Command Line Interface), and users will want a GUI (Graphical User Interface). An example of a good choice for a GUI would be a thin client using the HTTP protocol across an Intranet or the Internet. This ensures that anyone with a web browser can use the system, and it doesn't require vendor-dependent client software with software upgrades and rollouts to handle.
>
> Using the web as a front-end also ensures the client is platform-agnostic and works on Unix machines, Windows desktops, VMS hardware, Mac OS laptops, mobile phones, and all the many other variants around the world which support a web interface.
>
> Besides a GUI, users will probably also want an email interface, so that they can receive alerts about system activity, like when a ticket they submitted is resolved.

Ease of use
> The system should be easy to use. This means it should be intuitive to enter data, update the status, add interested parties, and assign scripts to certain events to modify the flow of a ticket to suit your particular requirements.

Multiuser
> The application needs to be able to handle more than one user at a time, both at the user level and at the administrator level. Any number of people in an organization must be able to enter data of people in an organization to enter data and open tickets at the same time. Equally, multiple administrators must be able to modify things like scripts and status flags at the same time, and not be needlessly restricted by waiting for someone else to complete their changes or logout before they can do any work. A help desk team, for example, may find themselves quite busy receiving, triaging, and resolving customer requests.

Ability to track history
> As previously mentioned, the system needs to be able to track not just the current state of an object but its entire modification history: who changed the status from *pending* to *resolved*, the original headers from the email (if the ticket came in an email), the IP address that created the ticket (if the ticket came from a web form), and so on.

Handling these things takes a lot of time and effort in the background. We use computers to make light work of tedious and repetitive tasks. Tracking the history of a ticket as it moves through the system is one of the many things that the system does for you. What part of the history is most relevant depends on your requirements, but the first step is to have the data.

Immutable history

Although tracking ticket history is essential, having a history of changes is not a lot of good to anyone if the history vanishes once a ticket is closed or finished in some manner. History must always be available and cannot be deleted erroneously.

Flexible views

The system should offer a means for viewing subsets of tickets: only the highest priority tickets, for instance. A user should be able to easily switch from viewing the open tickets for the last week, tickets that belong to a particular owner or user, tickets with a specific status, or those open for more than a minimum period of time, for example.

In addition, either the user or an administrator needs the ability to configure these views—add custom fields or alter the templates—for different user's needs.

Access control

It must be possible to control access, perhaps via an ACL (Access Control List) mechanism. Levels of access include who can view and alter the tickets, who can modify ticket status and priority, and who can assign interested parties. When the application includes the ability to write scripts or mini-programs to extend the functionality of the delivered system, the permissions to create and modify these and what they can do must be closely monitored and controlled. Perhaps different groups or queues need to have different access rights depending on their involvement in the task in question.

A ticketing system without an access control mechanism is a disaster waiting to happen.

Dependency management

The system needs a way to link tickets to one another and define dependencies. This makes it possible to set up linked lists or trees of events or status and prevent anyone from closing a particular ticket unitl all its dependencies are satisfied.

This is an important aspect of any true ticketing system. Without the ability to assign and follow dependencies and/or links to other tickets, there is no way to create meaningful workflow structures. In a naive system, it would be easy to miss relevant links and bypass entire tasks. With the ability to assign parent-child relationships to tasks, simple or complex dependencies can reflect the steps involved in a real process within a particular group or team.

Notifications

A ticketing system needs to be able to inform all parties of the current state of the tickets relevant to them. This sort of notification rule set centers around assigning users to groups, and users or groups to tickets.

Whenever the status of a ticket changes or some other defined event takes place, this is immediately reflected in the database for viewing via the thin client. Equally useful is the ability to send notification emails to any and all interested parties, or perhaps to execute a script which might notify people or programs in different ways. The possibilities are endless and simply need to be defined, based on the particular requirements of the people involved.

Customizable workflow

The system needs to be customizable to suit the requirements of the group using it. The company shouldn't have to change its procedures to accomodate a piece of inflexible software.

Deciphering the precise requirements of a client can be a difficult job. Specifications may be vague, misleading, or even downright wrong. One way around this is to allow the client to change the source code directly to accomodate their own requirements. This brings the power of a fully developed system to the hands of the people who actually use it and gives them the freedom to use it as they will.

Software is called *soft* for good reason—it should be flexible.

Ticketing Helps Everybody

Ticketing systems are good for multiple purposes and for many different people in different circumstances. Let's step back from the company or group perspective and look at how a ticket system benefits individuals.

What Ticketing Does for You

From a personal perspective, a ticketing system enables you to collect tasks in a list, assign a priority or status to it so the system can automatically order the list, and more or less forget about it until it's time to work on it. Deciding what to do next is simply a matter of looking up the most critical item and doing that task. The system decides on your behalf what is the most urgent task based on attributes you set.

A ticketing system also helps you manage your time more efficiently and avoid working on three or four things at once and not getting any of them done. You simply do the current task, mark it closed, and move on down the list. This is a bit like a shopping list: you can go to the checkout when everything on the list—the prerequisites for this shop—is in the basket. Once the checkout phase is complete, you move on to the next shop. Millions of people do this everyday, all around the world. They are using an unsophisticated ticketing system, the shopping list, which is ideal for a simple and solitary activity.

However, if you are involved in a large organization, you may work with a number of people from separate departments, and your job may involve multiple different tools and interrelated tasks. A ticketing system can simplify your complex and interrelated tasks to behave like a shopping list for your environment. Select an open ticket, work through the involved tasks, if there are any unfinished dependencies close them first, then close the parent ticket.

Divide and conquer, simplify and close.

What Ticketing Does for Your Team

Perhaps you manage a team of people, all working on vaguely related tasks. Each time a new task arrives for your department, you assign it to one or more people based on their apparent availability and skill set. The task may be a customer request, a production change, a system failure bug report or whatever it is that your department handles.

If you are using an effective ticketing system, you can easily find helpful information like the number of outstanding tasks, the status of all the submitted work this week, who is not overloaded, and who has more work than they can reasonably handle. You can locate essential tasks that are still open, and assign the merely nice-to-have tasks to the back-burner by simply changing the status of a ticket on a web page.

Members of your team can cross-assign tasks to other members when they're overworked, or find another team member who is more of an expert on a particular task. They can assign the expert to the ticket as an interested party or may even transfer ownership altogether.

This kind of system ensures high visibility. The entire team will always know the overall state of the tasks at hand—what needs doing and who should be doing it. Everyone will know who needs to pull their weight more and who is doing too much. There is always a balance to be found. This information will bring in, all by itself, peer pressure to get your list of tickets closed. Everyone will probably want to have closed the most tickets this week, particularly if this is tied to a bonus scheme. The bonus scheme may be targeted to the team, not necessarily to the individual, but the incentive and result remains the same—your team will become a more effective self-managing unit.

What Ticketing Does for Your Accountants

The accountants, or whoever watches the company profits, are essentially concerned with getting something for nothing or less.

A ticketing system will allow accountants to keep track of all the tasks requested from your group—a series of support requests, for example—and which tasks you've completed. They may be able to charge for each opened ticket, but they may only be able to charge a substantial sum or bonus for closed tickets, or for tickets closed within a specified period of time.

An automated tracking system enables accountants to make economic decisions based on real throughput of work, as well as to charge immediately for completed work, rather than waiting for this information to filter through an inefficient manual system. If the work is ticket-based, they could even automatically generate profit and loss forecasts based entirely on the contents of the ticketing system itself.

All of this makes a ticketing system a must for any bean-counter worth her salt.

What Ticketing Does for Your Boss

Your boss is not only responsible for giving work out to you and other employees. She must track the entire workforce, the work it is doing, and the outstanding work. She feeds reports back to her management in turn. Most bosses are only bosses relatively speaking, and report to higher management, shareholders, or their partners.

The boss provides summaries of the current state of progress, which go all the way up the food chain. The best way she can satisfy continual requests for status updates is to use the predefined views in the ticketing system to generate a suitable report. If these views are not sufficient, then the system needs to be able to produce flexible reports tailored to the relevant purpose.

Keeping your boss happy is an important part of a good ticketing system.

Getting Started

Although you may want a ticketing system because it will make handling and tracking tasks so much easier, the first step is to persuade the right people. You need enthusiasm for the solution across the organization.

Selling It to Management

The people who pay for it come first—management has to have an interest. They need to see the benefits for their business, their customers, and their bottom line.

Any of the points described in the section "Ticketing Helps Everybody" might help convince a manager that his workforce could be more productive with less resources. A ticketing system can help handle multiple requirements to ensure a smooth operation, save time, avoid missing tasks, prevent less critical work from impeding the important work, and make the entire workflow more efficient.

Last, implementing a ticketing system is an inexpensive solution with many rewards throughout an organization. It enables managers to track activity in a complex environment—knowledge is power.

Selling It to Staff

An enthusiastic manager is not enough, an excited staff is essential to the new process, too. One of the many reasons for individual members of a team to be keen on having a ticketing system in place is that they no longer need to inform a whole tree of people of the status of a particular chunk of work.

The familiar cries of: "Let me know when you've finished," "Don't interrupt me now, can't you see I'm busy,...," and "When you've done X, I'll tell you what to do next" need never be heard again. Once a ticketing system is in place, anyone in the team can pick up an outstanding piece of work with the highest priority and deal with it. They know no one else is going to start work on the task at the same time, because they are the *owner* of the task. No one needs to ask about progress, because everyone knows it is finished when the status is changed on the team web site. There may even be a customizable email to all interested parties. No more treading on each other's toes.

A ticketing system empowers the members of a team to handle discrete tasks with much less overhead and enables them to manage their own time more effieciently. Higher efficiency means less stress, less stress means happier staff, happy staff means a job well done, and we all go home early.

Getting People to Use the Ticketing System

Having a ticketing system is not enough—you need to use it! There are many ways to motivate people. Many implementors may think that the only choices are the *carrot* and the *stick*. An example of the carrot might be: "If you close more than 10 tickets a day, you can go home early." An example of the stick might be: "Unless you close more than 10 tickets a day, you're fired!"

Neither approach is ideal—both involve some authority figure who will either punish or reward performance. The carrot may even be an appropriate solution in some environments, but the danger is that it may promote unproductive competition between your team members. They may pick the easy-to-close tickets rather than the highest priority ones.

An alternative approach might be to educate the users of the ticketing system to appreciate the benefits of the improved workflow. This information does not need to focus solely on immediate improvements to the process, but it also might demonstrate how it will positively effect the provision of service, improve the confidence of the customer, and expand the bottom line of the firm. These lead to future expansion, more and better jobs, and perhaps world peace.

All of this depends on the nature of your work and your business model. You need to implement whatever solution works best for you. Each group may have to decide how to use the new tool to it's best advantage. Each situation will have its own best practice solution for local problems.

Why RT?

RT is designed not only to handle all the scenarios explored above, but it also is flexible enough to accomodate almost any variation with little or no specialized knowledge.

RT runs on a number of different mainstream platforms, including various flavors of Unix, Linux, Windows and Mac OS. RT supports several popular database backends: MySQL, PostgreSQL, and Oracle. Finally, RT uses Perl—a language familiar to many programmers and systems administrators—to make local customization easy.

RT also has a great user and developer community, with active email lists and a handy wiki (*http://wiki.bestpractical.com/*). And because RT is open source software, you are free to extend and change the core product to suit your needs.

This chapter has described what a succesful ticketing system needs to support a satisfied user base, without focusing on any particular tool or solution. The rest of this book gets down to the nitty-gritty and describes how to use RT itself, from typical installation scenarios to detailed configuration files, and from the commandline to the web-based GUI interface.

CHAPTER 2
Installation

Before you can make use of most of the wonderful advice and tricks in this book, you need a live RT instance running. If you already have an installed and running RT instance, skip to Chapter 3. In many ways, the initial installation of RT is the hardest part. RT is a complex Perl application with many dependencies—once all of those dependencies are in place, RT installs easily. Most of the time installing RT is spent installing those modules.

RT was designed to run on UNIX and UNIX-like systems. This means Linux, Solaris, FreeBSD, IRIX, HP/UX, Mac OS X, and similar systems. If your operating system of choice has pre-built packages for RT, that is the easiest way to install it. These third party packages are contributed and don't come from the RT developers. As of this writing, packages are available for Debian, FreeBSD, RedHat, and Mandrake Linux. There are some downsides to these packages: they may put files in unexpected locations to conform to packaging requirements, and they also may be out of date.

RT also runs on Windows. It is experimental and unsupported, so this chapter won't cover it, but it generally works. All of the component pieces (Perl, Apache, and MySQL) are available natively. The easiest way to get it running is to use Autrijus Tang's pre-packaged version of RT for Windows, which includes all the component pieces in one convenient installer. Download it from *http://wiki.bestpractical.com/ ?WindowsOSInstallGuide*.

Requirements

Before you begin setting up RT, you need to satisfy a few requirements. RT is complex, and the requirements are fairly strict, as Perl applications go.

Perl 5.8.3 or Later

You must have a recent version of Perl installed. RT will run on older versions of Perl, but bugs in the Unicode implementation in older versions may cause data corruption. (And you really don't want to have to explain that to your boss.)

You do not need to install the same Perl that you use for RT as your system-wide version of Perl (i.e., as */usr/bin/perl*). You can install it off to the side, in */usr/local* or wherever you'd like. If you choose to use mod_perl, it must be linked against this installation of Perl.

If the server running RT also runs other services (especially other mod_perl applications), you might want to create an installation of Perl specifically for RT to ensure that there are no dependency or version problems.

A Database

Ultimately, RT is all about its database. You have several options here:

- MySQL 4.0.14 or later, with InnoDB support enabled (*http://www.mysql.com/*)
- PostgreSQL 7.2 or later (*http://www.postgresql.com/*)
- Oracle 9iR2 or later (*http://www.oracle.com/*)
- SQLite (*http://www.sqlite.org/*)

RT runs equally well on MySQL and PostgreSQL. Oracle support is relatively new, but it should be as stable as the MySQL and PostgreSQL. An option for development is SQLite, a lightweight single-file database engine. We don't recommend you run it in a production environment, because it doesn't support high levels of concurrency well. Check the *README* file that comes with RT to see if the latest version supports any other databases.* You should choose which database to use based on what's familiar to you and what resources you have available.

If you don't have a preferred database, we suggest you choose MySQL. It is the easiest supported database to set up and maintain.

It may be possible to make RT install on earlier versions of MySQL or PostgreSQL, but as with earlier versions of Perl, you may run into trouble. In general, we recommend using the latest stable release version of whichever database you choose. At the time of writing, that version is MySQL 4.1.10 and PostgreSQL 8.0.1.

---

* As of this writing, Informix and Sybase support is being developed.

A Web Server

For production uses, you want a scalable web server (instead of the *standalone_httpd* that comes with RT). Any of the following will do:

- Apache 1.3 with mod_perl 1.x (*http://www.apache.org/* and *http://perl.apache.org/*)
- Apache 2.x with mod_perl 2.x
- Apache 1.x or 2.x with the FastCGI module (*http://www.fastcgi.com/*)
- Any FastCGI compliant web server

As with choice of database, choice of web server often depends on what you already have installed. If you're building a stand-alone RT system, the most stable configuration is the latest Apache 1.3 series release with the latest compatible mod_perl 1.x release.

At the time of this writing, mod_perl 2.0 has just been released. Some of the libraries that RT depends on haven't been put through their paces with it. During the mod_perl 2 beta cycle, most of the kinks have been worked out, but there could still be some gremlins hiding in the corners. (Make sure you build your Apache 2.0 with the prefork MPM to avoid odd threading issues.)

For more information on choosing between different Apache versions, you might want to look at *Apache: The Definitive Guide, 3rd Edition* (O'Reilly).

Most everyone runs RT on an Apache or Apache-derived web server, but RT's FastCGI server is known to play well with other servers. If you use something else, like SunOne/Netscape/iPlanet or WebStar and have a FastCGI plugin for it, it should work.

Perl Modules

RT makes heavy use of freely available Perl libraries available on the CPAN. To make your installation process somewhat smoother, Best Practical has created a (mostly) automated procedure using the CPAN.pm module to download and install libraries from CPAN. See "Step 6: Check for RT's Perl Dependencies" later in this chapter. Depending on your system configuration, there are still a couple of difficult modules that must be installed manually—mostly ones that require external libraries to be present, like your database's client libraries or the Apache libraries.

A list of required modules and versions can be found in Appendix D.

Standalone Server Mode

If you are just looking for a personal RT instance to play with, and don't plan to use it in production, you can use RT's Developer Mode—designed for quick and easy installation and startup.

This produces a totally self-contained RT instance in the directory the tar file was expanded in, will run as the current user.

First, download the latest tarball from *http://download.bestpractical.com/pub/rt/release/rt.tar.gz*. Untar it into a new directory.

Second, run *configure* with the appropriate arguments.

```
$ ./configure --with-my-user-group --with-db-type=SQLite \
    --enable-layout=inplace --with-devel-mode
```

Third, install all the necessary Perl dependencies.

```
$ make testdeps
$ make fixdeps
```

Finally, install.

```
$ make install
$ make initialize-database
```

Now, you can run the *standalone_httpd* and access your RT instance.

```
$ bin/standalone_httpd
HTTP::Server::Simple: You can connect to your server at http://localhost:8080/
```

Starting the Installation

Get yourself a comfortable chair, a nice drink, some free hard disk space, and sit down for an hour or so of module building and configuration to install RT.

Step 1: Choose a Machine and Location

Like most database driven applications, RT is relatively resource intensive, especially on RAM. The more memory you can afford to dedicate to RT and its database server, the snappier it will feel and the happier your users will be. Fast CPUs and disks will help as well.

Also in this step, you should install the appropriate webserver and database, if those aren't installed yet.

There are good O'Reilly books on each of the supported databases, including *Managing and Using MySQL*, *Practical PostgreSQL*, and *Oracle Essentials*. Many of these books are also available on Safari, O'Reilly's online library, which makes searching convenient. You can access Safari by going to *http://safari.oreilly.com*.

Step 2: Download the RT Source Tarball

You can find information about the latest RT releases from the official RT download page at *http://www.bestpractical.com/rt/download.html*. In addition to the locations for packaged releases, this page also contains instructions on how to download the latest development copy of RT.

The latest stable release of RT is always available as *http://download.bestpractical.com/pub/rt/release/rt.tar.gz*, so you can grab that now, and place it in */tmp*.

Step 3: Expand the tarball

With the tarball now in */tmp*, unpack it with *gunzip* or an equivalent utility on your system:

```
# gunzip -c rt.tar.gz | tar xvf -
```

This creates a directory named *rt-3.x.x*, where 3.x.x is the version of RT you downloaded. Make that directory your current working directory:

```
# cd rt-3.x.x
```

Take a moment to read through the *README* file in your new RT directory. This file covers the basics of the installation, with brief instructions on how to do the install. More importantly, this file is the canonical location for updates to the installation procedure. If you are using Oracle, you'll also want to read the Oracle-specific instructions in the file *README.Oracle*. Finally, any special notes about upgrading an RT installation are in the file *UPGRADING*.

Step 4: Prepare to Configure

At this point, you'll need to know certain information in order to continue: The server architecture (mod_perl 1.x, mod_perl 2.x, FastCGI); database type (MySQL, PostgreSQL, or Oracle); where the database lives and the usernames and passwords to access it; and which Perl you want to use. If you don't have that information yet, pause and collect it now.

Step 5: Configure the RT Installation Process

Now you need to tell RT how to install itself by running the *configure* program. It takes a number of different options. We'll explain most of them here and in the following sections, but you can get a complete and current list with the --help option:

```
# ./configure --help
```

General configuration

You can install RT in any directory by using the `--prefix` option, and it will put all of its files under that location. The default is */opt/rt3*. Some users prefer to specify */usr/local/rt3*. You can also put a private install in a location such as */home/you/projects/rt*.

```
--prefix=PREFIX        where to install RT's files to
```

Unless you change the configuration, RT will write any logs, session files, and HTML::Mason object cache files under the location you select, so you will want to choose a partition with a few hundred megabytes of free space.

Select alternate file layouts with `--enable-layout=inplace`, `--enable-layout=FHS`, and `--enable-layout=FreeBSD`. See *config.layout* in the source directory for more information on each.

File ownership configuration

These settings (see Table 2-1) control the file ownership that will be used on all of the installed files. You must make sure that all the users and groups exist before you try and configure RT. They are optional unless you wish to change the detected defaults.

Table 2-1. File ownership

Option	Meaning
`--with-rt-group=`*GROUP*	The group that owns all files (default: rt, rt3)
`--with-bin-owner=`*OWNER*	The user that owns the RT binaries (default: root)
`--with-libs-owner=`*OWNER*	The user that owns the RT libraries (default: root)
`--with-libs-group=`*GROUP*	The group that owns the RT libraries (default: bin)
`--with-web-user=`*USER*	The user the web server runs as (defaults: www, www-data, apache, httpd, nobody)
`--with-web-group=`*GROUP*	The group the web server runs as (defaults: www, www-data, apache, httpd, nogroup, nobody)
`--with-my-user-group`	Set all users and groups mentioned above to the current user and group (i.e. "you")

By default, RT assumes the existence of several users and groups on your system and will autodetect the defaults mentioned in this table. The standard configuration is to have all RT files owned by a 'rt' group. The installation process will chown or chgrp any files and directories that need to be accessible by the webserver.

These defaults are probably fine for most people installing into a system-wide directory like */opt/rt3* or */usr/local/rt3*. The reason for this complex set of permissions is because only certain users/groups should be able to write to (and read) certain files for security purposes.

On some systems, the web-user and web-group should be set to "nobody", "apache" or "httpd." Look at the User and Group lines in your httpd.conf for details.

If you are performing a non-root install, (i.e., into your home directory or entirely as a special rt user) then you can use --with-my-user-group to use only your current user and group. This will use the current value of the $USER or $LOGUSER environment variables and the first entry in the output of "groups".

Database configuration

RT needs to be able to talk to the database you've specified and also needs to create users and tables. To do this, it needs to know where you want your RT database to be. It also needs to know the username of an account that has permission to create and modify databases. For MySQL this is usually root but is configurable (see Table2-2). RT will prompt you for the administrator's password, so it can create the appropriate tables.

Table 2-2. Database options

Option	Meaning
--with-db-type=*TYPE*	The type of database RT will use: mysql, Pg, Oracle, SQLite or Informix (default: mysql)
--with-db-host=*HOSTNAME*	The fully qualified domain name of the database server (default: localhost)
--with-db-port=*PORT*	The port on which the database listens
--with-db-rt-host=*HOSTNAME*	The fully qualified domain name of RT server that talks to the database server (default: localhost)
--with-db-dba=*DBA*	The name of the database administrator (default: root)
--with-db-database=*DBNAME*	The name of the database to use (default: rt3)
--with-db-rt-user=*DBUSER*	The name of the database user (default: rt_user)
--with-db-rt-pass=*PASSWORD*	The password for the database user (default: rt_pass)

You will want to change the default password for the user RT will create. It's insecure to leave the default password of "rt_pass."

Perl configuration

Some systems have multiple instances or versions of Perl installed, and you don't always want to use the default one for RT. (This is especially true because RT requires a recent version of Perl to function properly.) Use the PERL environment variable to specify the location of the Perl binary you want RT to use. For example:

```
$ env PERL=/usr/local/bin/perl ./configure
checking for a BSD-compatible install... /usr/bin/install -c
checking for perl... /usr/local/bin/perl
checking for chosen layout... RT3
checking if user www exists... not found
checking if user www-data exists... not found
checking if user apache exists... found
checking if group www exists... not found
checking if group www-data exists... not found
```

```
checking if group apache exists... found
checking if group rt3 exists... not found
checking if group rt exists... found
checking if group apache exists... found
which: no apachectl in (/usr/local/bin:/bin:/usr/bin:/usr/X11R6/bin)
configure: creating ./config.status
config.status: creating sbin/rt-dump-database
config.status: creating sbin/rt-setup-database
config.status: creating sbin/rt-test-dependencies
config.status: creating bin/mason_handler.fcgi
config.status: creating bin/mason_handler.scgi
config.status: creating bin/standalone_httpd
config.status: creating bin/rt-crontool
config.status: creating bin/rt-mailgate
config.status: creating bin/rt
config.status: creating Makefile
config.status: creating etc/RT_Config.pm
config.status: creating lib/RT.pm
config.status: creating bin/mason_handler.svc
config.status: creating bin/webmux.pl
```

This shows a default configuration of RT, using the Perl binary located at */usr/local/bin/perl* and installing into the default location (*/opt/rt3*). Web scripts will be owned by the Apache user and in the Apache group. All other files will be in the rt group.

Step 6: Check for RT's Perl Dependencies

RT comes with a handy script called *rt-test-dependencies* that automatically queries your chosen version of Perl for all the modules that RT requires, and generates a report of what it finds. You can have RT run this script with the right options by issuing the following command:

```
# make testdeps
```

The script will output a report similar to the following:

```
/usr/local/bin/perl ./sbin/rt-test-dependencies --verbose --with-mysql
perl:
        5.8.3...found
users:
        rt group (apache)...found
        bin owner (root)...found
        libs owner (root)...found
        libs group (bin)...found
        web owner (apache)...found
        web group (apache)...found
MASON dependencies:
        Params::Validate 0.02...found
        Cache::Cache ...found
        Exception::Class 1.14...found
        HTML::Mason 1.23...found
        MLDBM ...found
        Errno ...found
```

```
          FreezeThaw ...found
          Digest::MD5 2.27...found
          CGI::Cookie 1.20...found
          Storable 2.08...found
          Apache::Session 1.53...found
          XML::RSS ...found
          HTTP::Server::Simple 0.07...MISSING
                  HTTP::Server::Simple version 0.07 required--this is only version 0.04
at (eval 41) line 2, <DATA> line 11.
          HTTP::Server::Simple::Mason 0.03...found
MAILGATE dependencies:
          HTML::TreeBuilder ...found
          HTML::FormatText ...found
          Getopt::Long ...found
          LWP::UserAgent ...found
CLI dependencies:
          Getopt::Long 2.24...found
CORE dependencies:
          Digest::base ...found
          Digest::MD5 2.27...found
          DBI 1.37...found
          Test::Inline ...found
          Class::ReturnValue 0.40...found
          DBIx::SearchBuilder 1.21...found
          Text::Template ...found
          File::Spec 0.8...found
          HTML::Entities ...found
          HTML::Scrubber 0.08...found
          Net::Domain ...found
          Log::Dispatch 2.0...found
          Locale::Maketext 1.06...found
          Locale::Maketext::Lexicon 0.32...found
          Locale::Maketext::Fuzzy ...found
          MIME::Entity 5.108...found
          Mail::Mailer 1.57...found
          Net::SMTP ...found
          Text::Wrapper ...found
          Time::ParseDate ...found
          Time::HiRes ...found
          File::Temp ...found
          Term::ReadKey ...found
          Text::Autoformat ...found
          Text::Quoted 1.3...found
          Tree::Simple 1.04...found
          Scalar::Util ...found
          Module::Versions::Report ...found
          Cache::Simple::TimedExpiry ...found
          XML::Simple ...found
DEV dependencies:
          Regexp::Common ...found
          Test::Inline ...found
          Apache::Test ...found
          HTML::Form ...found
          HTML::TokeParser ...found
```

```
        WWW::Mechanize ...found
        Test::WWW::Mechanize ...found
        Module::Refresh 0.03...found
MYSQL dependencies:
        DBD::mysql 2.1018...found
```

If anything is missing, RT can use the CPAN.pm module to install it. If you haven't previously configured CPAN.pm, you need to do that before running this script. Run `perl -MCPAN -eshell` and follow the instructions. Then, RT can attempt to automatically install the necessary modules; run `make fixdeps`:

```
# make fixdeps
```

This step requires either a network connection—to contact a CPAN mirror—or a local CPAN mirror, so that the installer can download any missing modules.

Earlier, you had the chance to specify three potentially different users and three groups: the user and group to own the scripts that RT installs, the user and group to own the libraries that RT installs, and the user and group that will run the web server process. At this point, you should make sure that these users and groups exist, because if they don't, the installation process will fail. How to do this depends on your system, but many systems provide the *useradd* and *groupadd* tools to automate the process. However you do it, create the users and groups now, if necessary.

Step 7: Install

RT will copy all the files to the appropriate location under PREFIX. If you are not doing a `--with-my-user-group` install, you will need to run this as root, since the process changes the ownership and permission of many of the files.

```
# make install
```

Step 8: Initialize the Database

RT will create the appropriate database, users, and initialize some tables when you run `make initialize-database` . (Do not run this more than once, unless you want to lose your data.)

```
# make initialize-database
Creating mysql database rt.
Now populating database schema.
Creating database schema.
schema sucessfully inserted
Now inserting database ACLs
Now inserting RT core system objects
Checking for existing system user...not found.  This appears to be a new
installation.
Creating system user...done.
Now inserting RT data
Creating Superuser  ACL...Creating groups...3.4.5.6.7.8.9.done.
Creating users...10.12.done.
Creating queues...1.2.done.
```

```
Creating ACL...2.3.done.
Creating ScripActions...1.2.3.4.5.6.7.8.9.10.11.12.13.14.15.done.
Creating ScripConditions...1.2.3.4.5.6.7.8.9.done.
Creating templates...1.2.3.4.5.6.7.8.9.10.11.12.done.
Creating scrips...1.2.3.4.5.6.7.8.9.10.11.12.13.done.
```

At this point, RT is installed. The next step is to configure it and then configure your web servers and mail servers to talk to it properly. If you already have a webserver with mod_perl or FastCGI set up, the hard work is over.

Upgrading RT

The process for applying minor version upgrades to RT is very similar to installing RT. You perform all the steps before `make install` as if you were performing a new installation, but you run `make upgrade` instead. Be sure to run a dependency check (step #6 earlier), as new versions of RT may require new versions of modules.

`make upgrade` will re-install RT files over your old files, but won't overwrite your local customizations or data—as long as you have followed the customization procedures in Chapter 8. Any other actions will be described in the *UPGRADING* file in the RT distribution.

Some upgrades require database changes. Usually these are just additions of new indexes or data. If you're performing such an upgrade, `make upgrade` will tell you how to run the appropriate files from *etc/upgrade/*.

If you're performing a major upgrade of RT that requires data conversion, such as from RT 2.x to 3.x, you'll need to follow the specific instructions documented in the *README* file.

Site Configuration

The primary configuration file for RT is *etc/RT_SiteConfig.pm*, which is based on *etc/RT_Config.pm*. You should *never* edit *etc/RT_Config.pm*. It contains default values and will get overwritten during upgrades. However, any changes you make in *etc/RT_SiteConfig.pm* will take precedence.

RT has many configuration options, but most sites only need a few to get up and running. For more advanced configuration options, see Chapter 7 and Appendix E.

The data in *RT_SiteConfig.pm* can be in any order. You should place things in logical groupings, so that you can easily find them. The definitive reference on the possible configuration options for any particular version of RT is *RT_Config.pm*.

Once you've finalized the configuration for your new RT instance, be sure to back up *RT_SiteConfig.pm* somewhere safe. Other than the database, this is the single most important file in your RT installation, and complex configurations can be difficult and time-consuming to recreate manually.

Site Details

There are some options you *must* configure. They are site-specific information.

The $rtname option is a short, unique name for this particular RT instance. It appears in the subject line of emails, so the RT instance can determine that the ticket was intended for it. Do not choose a generic name like "support" or "tech" for your $rtname, because this has the potential to conflict with other RT instances. A short version of your company name or its acronym are good examples.

```
Set($rtname, "examplecorp");
```

$Organization should be a unique identifier for this particular RT instance, similar to a domain-name. $Organization is used for generating message identifiers and linking between RT instances. It does not necessarily have to be a valid hostname.

```
Set($Organization, "rt.example.com");
```

Once you chose a $rtname and $Organization, you will need to be very careful about changing them, because RT uses them internally to maintain data structures.

Setting the $Timezone isn't required, but your users will be happier if you do. The value is system-specific. Look in your zoneinfo database directories (usually located in *usr/share/zoneinfo* or *usr/share/lib/zoneinfo*) for valid values.

```
Set($Timezone, 'US/Pacific');
```

You will also need to set $WebPath and $WebBaseURL to match how you will configure your webserver. $WebBaseURL should not have a trailing slash. $WebBaseURL includes the schema, hostname, and port (if necessary) for your RT instance. $WebPath is the rest of the path. An RT instance at *http://support.example.com/rt3* would use the following settings:

```
Set($WebBaseURL, "http://support.example.com");
Set($WebPath, "/rt3");
```

Or, an RT instance on its own virtualhost at *http://rt.example.com/* might use the following:

```
Set($WebBaseURL, "http://rt.example.com");
Set($WebPath, "/");
```

Email Configuration

RT needs to know the default addresses to use for queues that don't have an email address explicitly set. These must be configured in your mail system, as detailed later in this chapter.

```
Set($CorrespondAddress, 'correspond@rt.example.com');
Set($CommentAddress, 'comment@rt.example.com');
```

You may also need to tell RT how to send outbound email. Generally the default setting will work. If you don't have a sendmail-like program at */usr/sbin/sendmail*, you will need to set that path as appropriate. For example:

```
Set($SendmailPath, "/usr/lib/sendmail");
```

Logging

By default, RT logs all messages (level debug and up) to *syslog* with facility user. If you want to log to a file instead, use the following settings:

```
Set($LogToSyslog, '');                  # disable syslog
Set($LogToFile, 'debug');               # set file logging to include everything
Set($LogDir, '/opt/rt3/var/log');       # path to log
Set($LogToFileNamed , "rt.log");        # logfile name
```

Be sure to set the $LogDir appropriately.

Many more possibilities for logging configuration are discussed in Appendix E.

Sample RT_SiteConfig.pm

A sample site configuration might look like this:

```
Set($rtname, "examplecorp");
Set($Organization, "rt.example.com");
Set($Timezone, 'US/Pacific');
Set($WebBaseURL, "http://support.example.com");
Set($WebPath, "/rt3");
Set($CorrespondAddress, 'correspond@rt.example.com');
Set($CommentAddress, 'comment@rt.example.com');
Set($SendmailPath, "/usr/lib/sendmail");
Set($LogToSyslog, '');
Set($LogToFile, 'debug');
Set($LogDir, '/opt/rt3/var/log');
Set($LogToFileNamed , "rt.log");
Set($OwnerEmail, "admin@example.com");
Set($MyTicketsLength, 20);
1;
```

Configuring Your Web Server

Now that you have RT configured, it is time to configure your webserver. In the previous stage you set $WebBaseURL and $WebPath to where in "URLspace" you plan to have RT installed. Now we'll tell Apache about those values. (If you are not using Apache, you will need to extrapolate from the FastCGI section below.)

Apache and mod_perl

A common configuration for RT is to place it on its own VirtualHost, such as on *rt.example.com* for the *example.com* organization.

Use the following configuration in your httpd.conf:

```
<VirtualHost *>
    ServerName rt.example.com
    DocumentRoot /opt/rt3/share/html
    AddDefaultCharset UTF-8

    PerlModule Apache::DBI
    PerlRequire /opt/rt3/bin/webmux.pl

    <Location />
        SetHandler perl-script
        PerlHandler RT::Mason
    </Location>
</VirtualHost>
```

You will need `NameVirtualHost` * earlier in your *httpd.conf* unless you are using IP-based virtual hosting. (In that case, specify an IP address in place of the *.)

That configuration corresponds to the following lines in *RT_SiteConfig.pm*.

```
Set($WebBaseURL, "http://rt.example.com");
Set($WebPath, "/");
```

Using a separate virtual host isn't required. You can place RT at any location on your webserver. The following example places it at /rt3/:

```
Alias /rt3 /opt/rt3/share/html
<Location /rt3>
    AddDefaultCharset UTF-8
    SetHandler perl-script
    PerlHandler RT::Mason
    PerlModule Apache::DBI
    PerlRequire /opt/rt3/bin/webmux.pl
</Location>
```

If your webserver is *www.example.com*, these would be the *RT_SiteConfig.pm* entries:

```
Set($WebBaseURL, "http://www.example.com");
Set($WebPath, "/rt3");
```

mod_perl 1.x v. mod_perl 2.x

In choosing between mod_perl 1.x and 2.x, there are no hard and fast rules. mod_perl 1.x is several years old and is known to be very stable. mod_perl 2.x is cleaner, faster, and sits on top of the more powerful Apache 2 core.

FastCGI

An alternative to mod_perl is FastCGI. FastCGI is a protocol designed to allow a web server to run CGI scripts via a separate, persistent program. FastCGI defines how a web server interacts with this separate program in much the same way that the

CGI spec defines how a web server and regular spawned programs interact. There are FastCGI implementations for many web servers—including Apache 1.3.x and Apache 2.x—that should work just fine with RT.

There are several cases where you might want to use FastCGI instead of mod_perl:

- FastCGI is much simpler to install; mod_perl may be difficult to build on some systems.
- Your core Apache process will stay small in size.
- Because the perl process running RT is a separate process, it can be stopped or restarted without having to take down the web server.
- FastCGI programs are often easier to manage, both for sysadmins maintaining a running instance and for developers who are making frequent changes to their code.

The official FastCGI homepage is at *http://www.fastcgi.com/*, and it provides a lot of good information about running and developing FastCGI applications, as well as download information.

Configuring FastCGI under Apache, you'll need this chunk of configuration in your *httpd.conf*:

Under Apache, as a separate virtual host, the configuration looks like this:

```
<VirtualHost *>
  ServerName rt.example.com

  FastCgiServer /opt/rt3/bin/mason_handler.fcgi
  AddHandler fastcgi-script fcgi
  Alias /NoAuth/images/ /opt/rt3/html/NoAuth/images/
  ScriptAlias / /opt/rt3/bin/mason_handler.fcgi/
</VirtualHost>
```

If your RT will live at /rt3/, the configuration would look like this:

```
FastCgiServer /opt/rt3/bin/mason_handler.fcgi
AddHandler fastcgi-script fcgi
Alias /rt3/NoAuth/images/ /opt/rt3/html/NoAuth/images/
ScriptAlias /rt3 /opt/rt3/bin/mason_handler.fcgi/
```

By default, FastCGI will start only one process at a time. If your RT instance experiences high concurrent use, you will want to tell FastCGI to start more processes by using the -processes option to FastCgiServer.

```
FastCgiServer /opt/rt3/bin/mason_handler.fcgi -processes 10
```

Serving RT Behind a Proxy Webserver

Depending on your configuration, you might not be able to, or want to, run RT on your main webserver. One solution to this problem is to use a proxy in front of it.

Figure 2-1 shows a proxied RT server. Apache 2.x, beyond being a webserver, also can function as a high-performance proxy.

There are several reasons you might want to do this:

First, only one instance of a mod_perl 1.x application can run inside Apache at a time, because there is a shared Perl interpreter. Multiple instances of an application can conflict with unexpected and undesirable results. A proxy can be used to map multiple instances into one URLspace.

Apache 2.x and mod_perl 2.x doesn't have this limitation. Perl interpreters can be bound to VirtualHosts or Locations with `PerlOptions +Parent`.

Second, Perl applications use a lot of RAM, and all Apache processes will end up allocating this RAM. If you also are serving static content, the memory usage will be high, thus limiting the number of Apache processes a machine can support and throughput..

Third, a proxy can allow your server to serve more requests. The back-end server won't need to buffer for a slow network connection and can quickly return to serving requests. This means you will need fewer heavy mod_perl processes running.

Finally, RT is designed to be a secure application, but as with any piece of software there is always potential for a hole to be found. By using a proxy to a dedicated Apache server, RT can be isolated from other services on the system. A compromise of RT would not imply instant access to the rest of the web system.

Apache 2.x is a good candidate for this, as it's a bit faster and a little more flexible than Apache 1.x.

In your front-end proxy webserver, use the following configuration, after making sure that `mod_rewrite` and mod-proxy loaded:

```
<VirtualHost *>
    ServerName rt.example.com
    RewriteEngine On
    RewriteRule ^/(.*)$ http://localhost:8284/$1 [P,L]
</VirtualHost>
```

Under Apache 2.x, `mod_proxy` offers a cleaner configuration:

```
<VirtualHost *>
    ServerName rt.example.com
    ProxyPass / http://localhost:8284/
    ProxyPassReverse / http://localhost:8284/
</VirtualHost>
```

Then, as shown in Figure 2-1, configure another Apache running RT on a high-numbered port, such as 8284 in this example. You can configure your firewall so it can only receive traffic from the proxy server.

This approach is explained in great detail in the mod_perl documentation, at *http://perl.apache.org/docs/1.0/guide/strategy.html*, and in the mod_perl Developer's Cookbook, by Geoffrey Young, Paul Lindner, and Randy Kobes (Sams) and in *Practical mod_perl* by Stas Bekman and Eric Cholet (O'Reilly).

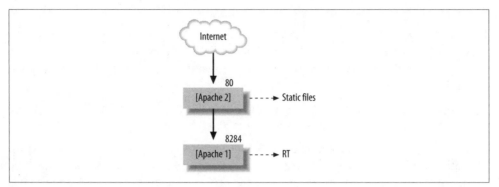

Figure 2-1. Proxied RT server

Standalone Server

RT also includes a standalone webserver. It doesn't need Apache or anything besides Perl and RT.

You can start it by running `bin/standalone_httpd`. You may also specify a port number, i.e. `bin/standalone_httpd 8888`.

The standalone server is meant primarily for development. It can do only one thing at a time, which makes it suboptimal for multiple concurrent users.

Configuring Outbound Email

Configuring RT to send mail consists of a few steps. First of all, make sure that the server has a working MTA (Mail Transfer Agent).

Common MTAs include sendmail (*http://www.sendmail.org/*), postfix (*http://www.postfix.org/*), and qmail (*http://cr.yp.to/qmail.html*). Most Unix-based operating systems ship with at least one of these available by default (Linux distributions have almost all of them available, in fact). Installing and configuring the MTA is beyond the scope of this book, but the vendors' web sites all provide detailed installation and configuration instructions.

Once you have the MTA installed and set up to send mail, you need to tell RT to use it. Look in the *RT_Config.pm* file, and copy the following lines to *RT_SiteConfig.pm*:

```
Set($SendmailPath , "/usr/sbin/sendmail");
Set($SendmailArguments , "-oi -t");
```

Since it's the traditional location for sendmail, */usr/sbin/sendmail* will usually work. Most other MTAs respect this tradition through compatibility wrappers. If */usr/sbin/sendmail* does not exist, try */usr/lib/sendmail*.

Configuring Inbound Email

Incoming mail destined for RT is processed through RT's mailgate, conveniently called *rt-mailgate*. When it is invoked, this script parses the incoming message, and transfers it to your main RT server for processing. The mailgate does not have to run on the same machine as your main RT server, as long as it can communicate with it via http or https.

MTAs have the ability to pass mail destined for particular addresses to a program instead of to a mailbox, and RT utilizes this. Unfortunately, this feature is configured differently for different MTAs. Most of them support Sendmail's traditional *aliases* format, so that's the format we'll be using for the examples in the following sections. A notable exception is qmail, which will be covered separately.

Mailgate Options

Several different command line options are supported by rt-mailgate (as shown in Table 2-3).

Table 2-3. Mailgate options

Option	Meaning
--action=*comment*/correspond	Select whether this email should be processed as a comment or correspondence.
--queue=**QUEUENAME**	Select which queue to process the email into.
--url=**URL OF RT INSTANCE**	The URL of your RT instance.
--debug	Print debugging messages.
--extension=queue|action|ticket	Select the Queue, Action, or Ticket to operate on based on the $EXTENSION environment variable. For systems like Sendmail and Postfix which support rt+extension@host notation.
--timeout=*SECONDS*	How many seconds to give up after. Defaults to 180.

Using the mailgate with Sendmail or Postfix

Sendmail's */etc/aliases* file uses a simple name: value format, with the address receiving the mail on the left of the colon and the address to which it expands on the right hand side. The expansion address can be one of a few different types, including a different email address, a filename, or a program. There can be several expansion addresses as well, separated by commas.* You must run the newaliases command after editing */etc/aliases*.

To specify a program to run when mail comes to an address you can use this syntax:

```
correspond: "|/opt/rt3/bin/rt-mailgate --queue General --action correspond --url
http://rt.example.com/"
```

---

* This is a very simple way to implement mailing lists.

This passes the message to the script */opt/rt3/bin/rt-mailgate*, which is configured with the command line arguments following the script name.

Modern versions of Sendmail require all programs called from the */etc/aliases* file to be symlinked into the */etc/smrsh/* directory. You will receive `DSN: Service unavailable` errors if you haven't done this. Use the following command:

```
# ln -s /opt/rt3/bin/rt-mailgate /etc/smrsh/
```

Postfix sometimes stores its *aliases* file at */etc/postfix/aliases*. This file is in the same format as Sendmail's. After editing it you must run Postfix's `newaliases` script.

Using the mailgate with qmail

Unlike Sendmail and Postfix, qmail uses specially-named files in a user's home directory to determine the handler for a message. Since you have already created a user account for RT, you can set that user up to process all RT-related mail. When qmail's delivery agent tries to figure out what to do with an incoming message for a user, it first looks to see if there is an extension to the username. By default, this extension is separated from the username by a dash (-), so you could have `rt-foo@rt.example.com`, where `rt` is the username and `foo` is the extension. If there is an extension, then qmail will look in the `rt` user's *~/.qmail-foo* file for delivery instructions. Otherwise, it looks in the `rt` user's *~/.qmail* file.

To set up mail delivery into RT, you can create a series of *.qmail* files, two for each queue (for responses and comments). For example, the General queue would be handled by these files:

```
# cat ~rt/.qmail-general
|/opt/rt3/bin/rt-mailgate --queue General --action correspond --url http://rt.
example.com/

# cat ~rt/.qmail-general-comment
|/opt/rt3/bin/rt-mailgate --queue General --action comment --url http://rt.example.
com/
```

With these files in place, mail sent to *rt-general@rt.example.com* will become correspondence in the General queue, and mail sent to *rt-general-comment@rt.example.com* will become comments in the General queue.

You also can create a catch-all *.qmail-default* file:

```
# cat ~rt/.qmail-default
|/opt/rt3/bin/rt-mailgate --queue $DEFAULT --action correspond --url http://rt.
example.com/
```

Anything sent to `rt-queuename` will be delivered as correspondence to the `queuename` queue.

Note the `rt-` at the beginning of each address; that is because the mail is actually being sent to the `rt` user and handled using qmail's convenient features. Setting up qmail so that these messages are handled globally, and not by a particular user, is a little different. Rather than a global *etc/aliases* file, like the other MTAs use, qmail has a general `alias` user that handles all system-wide aliases. To make this user handle mail for RT, simply create the files *~alias/.qmail-general* and *~alias/.qmail-general-comment* with the same content as before. This allows the RT addresses to be general@rt.example.com and general-comments@rt.example.com. Under RT2, the mail handling script had to be setgid to the rt group, so the user restriction was important, but under RT3, this is no longer the case.

Using the mailgate with procmail

You also can call the mailgate from procmail. This allows you to perform virus or spam filtering before mail gets to RT. This can be very important because RT addresses are often published in places where spam-crawlers can find them.

Here's an example procmail file that performs spam and virus filtering with Spam-Assassin and ClamAV:

```
CLAMSCAN=`/usr/bin/clamscan --mbox --disable-summary --stdout -`

:0 iD
* CLAMSCAN ?? FOUND
viruses

:0fw
| spamassassin

:0 H
* ^X-Spam-Status: Yes
spam

:0
* ^TO_rt-general@
| /opt/rt3/bin/rt-mailgate --queue general --action correspond --url http://rt.
example.com/

:0
* ^TO_rt-general-comment@
| /opt/rt3/bin/rt-mailgate --queue general --action comment --url http://rt.example.
com/
```

This file will send all messages to *rt-general@rt.example.com* to the general queue as correspondence, and all messages to *rt-general-comment@rt.example.com* to the general queue as a comment. With a little bit of procmail magic, you can do much more powerful filtering and mail direction, but that's beyond the scope of this book.

For more information on procmail, try *The Procmail Companion* (Addison Wesley), or visit *http://procmail.org/* for more procmail resources.

Installation Problems

Not everyone's installation goes perfectly the first time. There are some common problems that may occur.

- All necessary Perl dependencies must be installed. Make sure you've run `configure` with the proper arguments followed by a `make testdeps`. If there are any failures, you will need to resolve them.

- If you have odd email issues, double check that you have configured Sendmail's smrsh by symlinking */opt/rt3/bin/rt-mailgate* into */etc/smrsh*.

Some places to go for help are the `rt-users` mailing list on *http://lists.bestpractical.com*, Chapter 8, or the RT Wiki at *http://wiki.bestpractical.com*.

Installation Complete

At this point you should have a working RT instance. Restart your Apache, and test it out by pointing your web browser at whatever URL you've specified.

The default administrator user for RT is called `root` and the password is `password`. After you log in for the first time, you will want to change this by clicking on "Preferences" in the upper right hand corner.

## CHAPTER 3

Getting Started

In this chapter, we'll give you a basic overview of how to use RT's web interface. This is the primary interface to RT for both users and administrators—you can access all of RT's features and configuration options through it. Once you've read this chapter you should be able to log into RT and find, modify, and resolve tickets. We'll also touch on what you can use email for and how it integrates with RT. The RT command-line tool, covered in Chapter 4, also performs many of the same tasks you'll learn in this chapter.

This chapter assumes that you are running your own RT installation. If you are using an existing installation to learn about RT, be careful about creating new tickets. You don't want to broadcast your test tickets inadvertently to the entire user base. For experimenting, you might be interested in the standalone server that ships with RT. The standalone server is a small web server written in Perl. Because it can handle only a limited number of concurrent web clients, it is not really suitable for anything other than testing. However, it is very useful for that, because it requires no other web server to be installed. See the sidebar "Standalone Server Mode" in Chapter 2 for instructions on how to start the standalone server.

Logging in to RT

If you are working in an environment where there is an existing RT installation, your RT administrator most likely will give you a username and password as well as instructions on where the RT login URL is. When you first connect, you will see a login box, something like the one in Figure 3-1.

If you have a brand new RT instance, you can log in with the default username *root* and password *password*. You should change this password immediately by clicking on the Preferences link, especially if your RT instance is accessible from the Internet.

Once you've successfully authenticated yourself to RT, you will see the home page with the title "RT at a glance." This page, shown in Figure 3-2, displays a snapshot

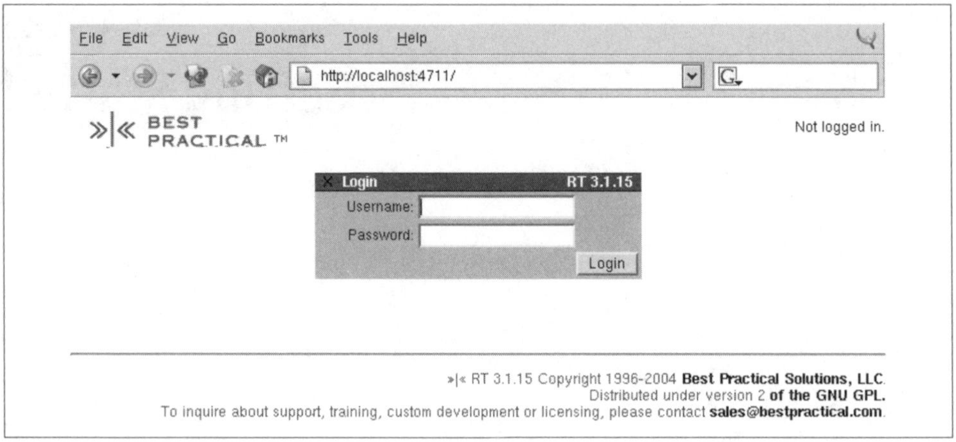

Figure 3-1. RT login box

of RT as it applies to you. It gives you easy access to the tickets you own, tickets you've requested, tickets in the queues you watch, and interfaces for finding existing tickets and creating new ones. Many items on this page are clickable—such as ticket numbers, ticket summaries, and queues—and take you to ticket displays or queue listings.

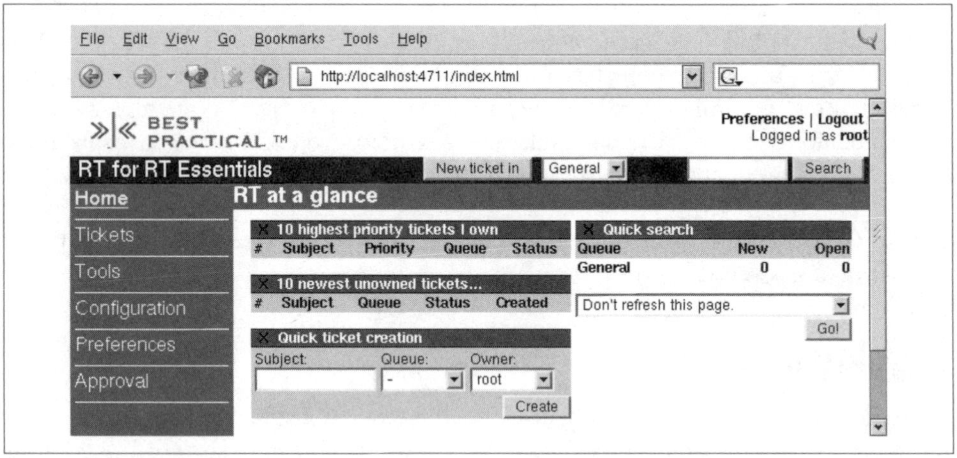

Figure 3-2. RT at a glance

The display is easy to customize and extend, so don't be too alarmed if what you see is not exactly the same as what these screenshots show. Since this home page is intended to be a clearinghouse of information, administrators may add extra queue displays or links to documentation, internal policies, and canned searches. The next major release of RT should make this sort of configuration.

Along the left side of the page is the main site menu. This menu has links to all of the major things you can do with RT: search for tickets, configure RT, change your preferences, and so on. Configuration is covered in more depth in Chapter 5, and customizing your preferences will be covered in Chapter 6. The rest of this chapter concentrates on the Tickets menu item.

Creating a New Ticket

You can create a ticket from anywhere in RT; the top of every page has a small form with a button labeled *New Ticket in* and a drop-down menu listing the queues you can access. Select the queue in which you want to create a new ticket, and click the New Ticket in button. It will take you to the new ticket form shown in Figure 3-3.

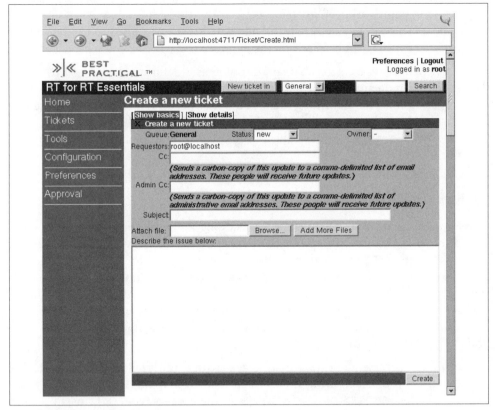

Figure 3-3. Create a new ticket (basic)

The two most important fields in this basic form are the subject of the ticket and an entry box for a description; these are the first items that people see when they look at your ticket. The subject is displayed on the main page with no context, so you should make sure that it is clear and concise. The description field is the primary explanation for what the ticket is about, so you should take care to include all the relevant information. Also keep in mind how the description will be used. For example, tickets created in an Emergency queue outside of business hours might send a message to the on-call operator's SMS device. A ticket that does not get to the point within the SMS character limit will be pretty frustrating for everyone involved.

Fill in all the appropriate details, click the Create button, and you'll have a new ticket. Congratulations!

There is a quick ticket creation box at the bottom of the home page that instantly creates a new ticket with an empty description.

Tickets are identified by number. On a fresh install, the first ticket you create is numbered 1. Every new ticket after that gets a number one higher than the previous ticket. If your RT instance is configured to send mail when a ticket is created (as it is by default), then you should get an email message shortly with a summary of the ticket you created. This message tells you the number that was assigned to the new ticket and provides a URL to the ticket display form. Keep this URL, as you'll need it shortly.

When a new ticket is created, RT may run some user-defined actions—called *scrips*. These scrips can do almost anything, but the most common type of scrip sends mail to the queue's watchers informing them of the new ticket. Other scrips might send a notification to an alphanumeric pager, post a message to an IRC channel, or even print the ticket's info to a local line printer. You can read more about scrips in Chapter 5.

Ticket Display Page

The important part of handling a request is doing the work, but once you've completed the task, you need to update the ticket to reflect your work. So how do you update a ticket? First, you need to go the main display page for that ticket. Clicking on a ticket's ID or Subject from the home page (Figure 3-2) is one way to get there. If you click on the name of a queue in the Quick Search box on the right of the home page, you can preview all the tickets in that queue and select your ticket from the list. You also can enter a ticket number in the search box on the top right of every page, and click Search to get there.

A fourth way to get to the ticket display page is with a direct link in the browser. The URL to display a ticket always will be in the format *http://<RTSERVER>/Ticket/ Display.html?id=<NUMBER>*, where *RTSERVER* is the root of your RT instance, and *NUMBER* is the ID of the ticket. The notification emails RT sends when a new ticket is created will contain this URL unless your administrator has removed it from the template. If none of these help you, and you don't know the ticket number, you can use the search interface to find your ticket. RT's search UI lets you build complex queries with relative ease; see "Searching for Tickets" later in this chapter.

BUSINESS REPLY MAIL

FIRST-CLASS MAIL   PERMIT NO. 80   SEBASTOPOL CA

Postage will be paid by addressee

O'REILLY MEDIA INC.
BOOK REGISTRATION
1005 GRAVENSTEIN HIGHWAY NORTH
SEBASTOPOL CA 95472-9910

Register Your O'Reilly Book!

oreilly.com/go/register

Register your books to receive important updates, upgrade offers and our catalog. Go to *oreilly.com/go/register*, or complete and return this postage paid card.

Name _____

Company/Organization _____

Address _____

City _____ State _____ Zip/Postal Code _____ Country _____

Email address _____ Telephone _____

Book Title _____ ISBN # _____

Book Title _____ ISBN # _____

Book Title _____ ISBN # _____

Book Title _____ ISBN # _____

oreilly.com/go/register

Part #30031

Once you get to the ticket's display page, you are confronted with a colorful interface, which shows the major groups of ticket attributes. The metadata associated with a ticket is divided into four main categories—Basics, Dates, People, and Links—each of which tracks a different aspect of the ticket, as in Figure 3-4. You can edit each category individually by clicking on the category name in the main display area or by clicking on the category link in the sidebar on the left. The Jumbo form linked from the sidebar edits all attributes at once. The Jumbo form is quite busy compared to the other pages, but it has the advantage of allowing many different types of updates all at once.

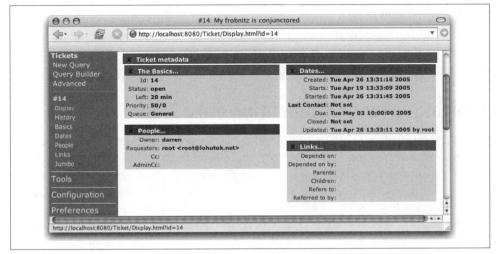

Figure 3-4. Ticket display

The Basics category includes obvious things, like the subject, status, priority, and queue of a ticket. It also includes elements like the estimated amount of time to complete the work, the amount of time worked on the ticket—which can be very useful for tracking the scale of requests—and the amount of time left before the initial estimated completion date passes. This area displays any custom fields attached to the ticket as well.

The Dates category includes the start date of the ticket, the date the actual work started, when the requestor was last contacted about the request, and the date by which the work must be completed. If you and other users maintain these dates accurately, they can be used to generate reports on how long requests take to be fulfilled. Dates can be entered in a variety of formats, and, as long as the format is unambiguous, RT will figure it out.

The People category lists watchers, requestors, and the ticket's owner. Long-lived tickets have a tendency to accumulate many watchers over time, as more man-power is added to fulfilling a request and managers of various sorts start getting interested in why the request is taking so long to be finished. The form to edit a ticket's People data functions as a search form as well as a modification form. It can find users and groups in RT based on simple searches, remove watchers from the ticket, and change the owner of the ticket by changing the value in the Owner drop-down menu.

The Links category contains all the links between the current ticket, other tickets, and the outside world. You can merge tickets and link them with other tickets through this form. See "Merging Duplicate Tickets" and "Associating Related Tickets" later in this chapter for more details.

Beneath the blocks of metadata on the ticket display page is the ticket's history. This is an audit trail—each ticket update (transaction) has its own place in this list, from the initial creation to every attribute change, reply, or comment.

Many of these transactions record outgoing email. These emails are individually viewable in their entirety, including all of RT's special headers and headers that are not normally passed on to mail clients, such as Bcc.

Replying to (and Commenting on) a Ticket

RT records two main types of transactions: attribute changes and correspondence. Correspondence and comments are what adds content to a ticket and covers all the replies and user feedback that RT collects. While you can change many different types of attributes, most of the interesting content in your RT installation will come from correspondence. Comments are generally intended as private or internal correspondence about a ticket. RT is very flexible and the exact mechanics will depend on how your administrator has configured RT, but usually correspondence is visible to end-users and comments are not.

You reply to a ticket by clicking the Reply link at the top right of the ticket display page or beside an individual item in the ticket's history. Figure 3-5 shows the form for responding to tickets. The same form creates either replies or comments, depending on what you select for Update Type. From this form, it's simple to reply to an end user, mark down how much time you spent composing your response, and close the ticket.

Escalating a Ticket

Each ticket has a priority. Priority is a way to indicate relative importance. It can be any integer. Most organizations use the range 0-100. Every queue has a default priority for new tickets if you don't explicitly set one. To escalate the priority of a ticket, set the priority of a ticket to a higher number. The priority field is in the Basics category, shown in Figure 3-6.

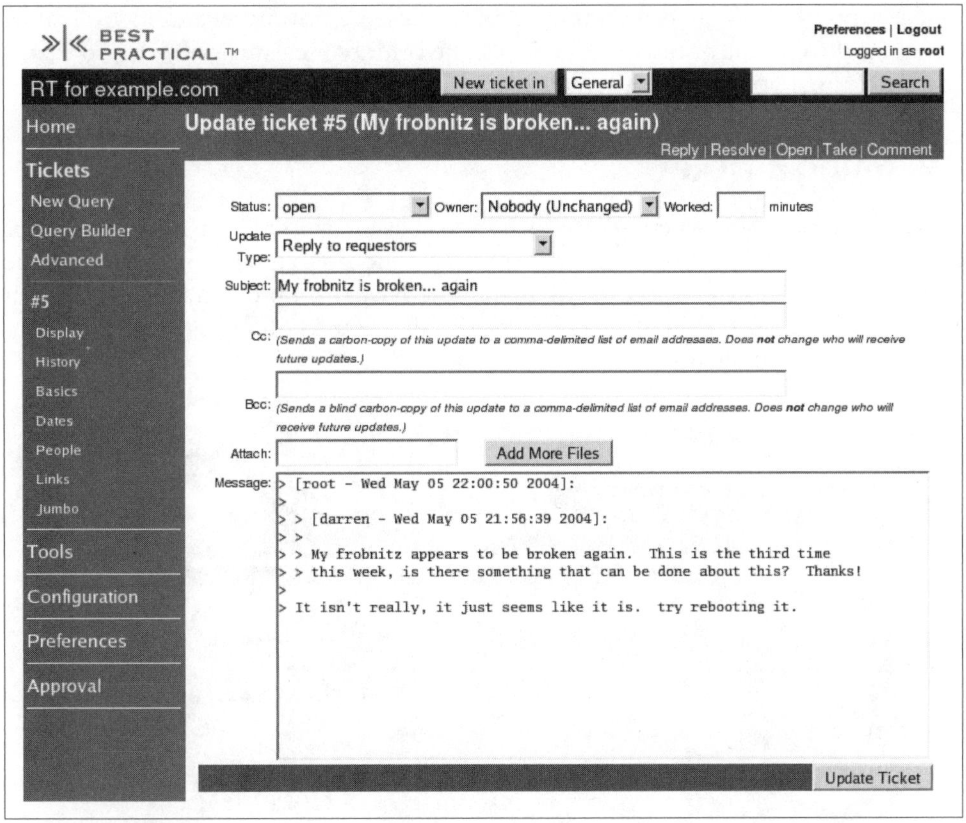

Figure 3-5. Ticket reply

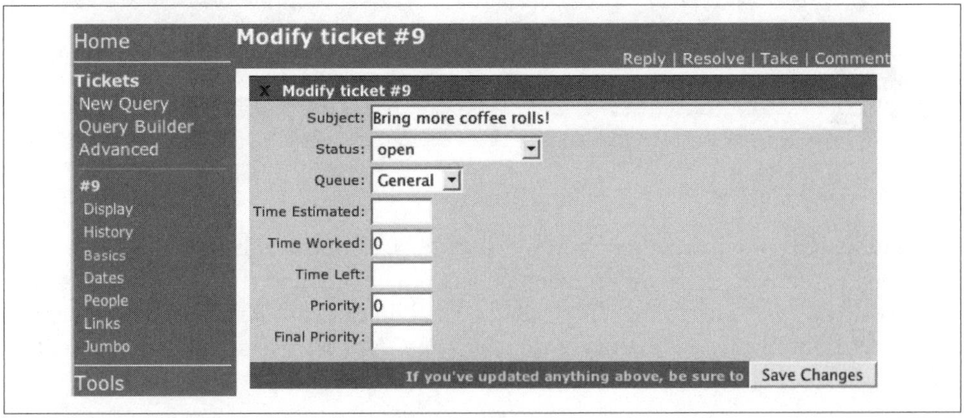

Figure 3-6. Ticket priority

Queues can be configured to automatically adjust the priority of tickets over time. Based on the current priority of the ticket, the priority escalates every day so that it reaches its final priority on a given due date.*

Assigning a Ticket

Tickets can have an owner—the user responsible for working on the ticket or for coordinating the work. To assign a ticket to someone, go to the People form from the ticket display page, and select the user from the Owner drop-down list, as shown in Figure 3-7. This list contains the usernames of all the users allowed to own tickets in the ticket's current queue.

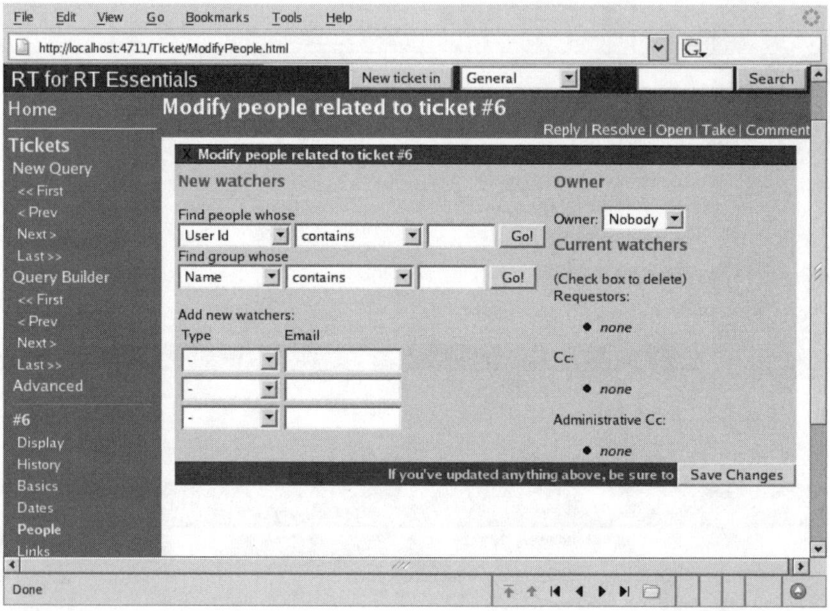

Figure 3-7. Assigning a ticket

You can assign only tickets that you own or that are unowned. If you need to reassign a ticket that you do not own, you can steal the ticket and then assign it to someone else. Tickets you can steal will display a Steal link next to Reply and Comment in the upper right corner of the ticket display page. Not all users have access to steal tickets, see "ACL" in Chapter 8.

---

* Your RT administrator needs to enable automatic escalation using *rt-crontool*.

Resolving a Ticket

When you are satisfied that the ticket you are working on is finished, you can change its status to resolved, so other users know it doesn't need any more work. This process is known as resolving the ticket. To modify a ticket's status, just click *Resolve* in the upper right hand corner of any ticket page, as shown in Figure 3-8.

The form used for resolving a ticket allows you to send a reply to the ticket's requestor and watchers.

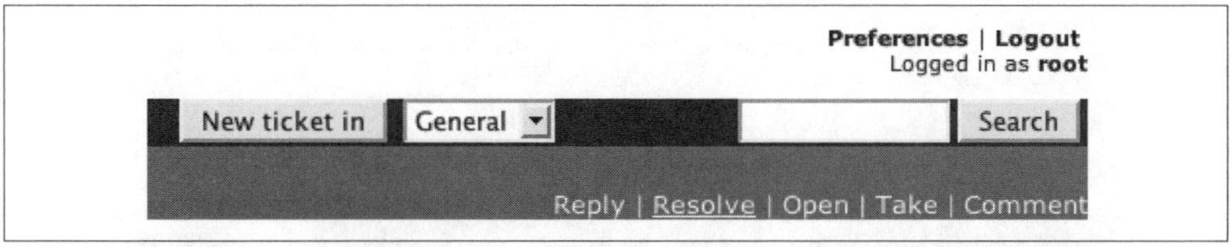

Figure 3-8. Resolving a ticket

Certain scrips run when a ticket is resolved. The default scrips send mail to the ticket's watchers.

Merging Duplicate Tickets

Sometimes, multiple people submit reports for the same problem. This is especially likely if you've got a big problem in a busy environment. When it happens, you need a way to tell RT that the multiple tickets are actually the same request. RT lets you collapse tickets together in a process called *Merging*.

Go to the Links form for the ticket you want to merge. This form has two major sections, Current Links and New Links, as shown in Figure 3-9. The Current Links section describes any existing relationships that the ticket has and provides a simple editing interface. The New Links section allows you to define new relationships.

To merge one ticket into another, enter the number of the target ticket in the Merge Into Field, and submit the form. You can merge any number of tickets this way, although you need to merge them one at a time.

Once the tickets are merged, displaying either ticket number will display the metadata and history for all the merged tickets. Any further changes to any of the merged tickets also will show up on all the merged tickets. Figure 3-10 shows the merge transaction in the status listing of a merged ticket.

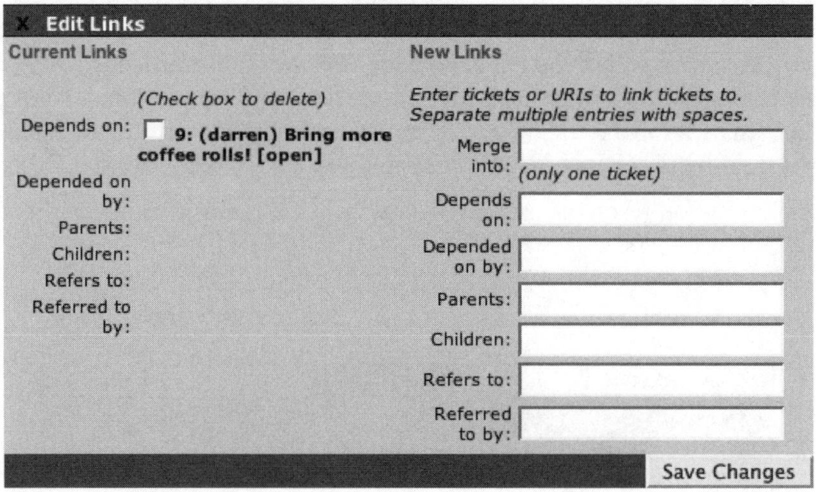

Figure 3-9. Ticket links form

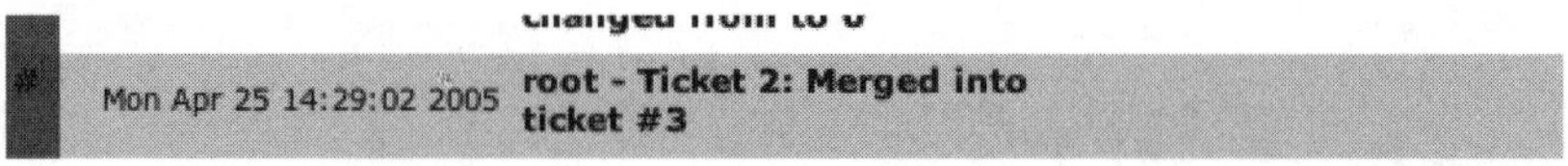

Figure 3-10. Merge transaction in ticket status

Associating Related Tickets

Sometimes a ticket represents a complex issue or difficult request, and you may need to break it down into smaller, more manageable pieces. When this happens, it makes sense to create tickets for these smaller tasks, and associate them with the original ticket. RT provides a *Depends On/Depended On By* relationship for these cases. From the Links form of the new ticket, shown in Figure 3-8, enter the original ticket's number in the *Depended On By* field, and save your changes.

You can create this relationship from the other direction as well: on the Links form for the original ticket you can enter the new ticket's number in the Depends On field. Once this relationship is established, the parent ticket cannot be resolved until the child ticket is resolved. A ticket can have multiple parents and multiple children, which can be used to create arbitrarily complex and interdependent workflows.

The *Depends On/Depended On By* relationships are similar to the parent and child relationships. The practical difference is that RT doesn't enforce the relationships. With parent/child relationships, the parent ticket cannot be resolved until all the child tickets are resolved, but with *Depends On/Depended On By* relationships, either ticket can be resolved without the other.

Sometimes tickets are not directly related, but mention other tickets. For example, a ticket about email slowness might mention a ticket from earlier that morning about the Exchange server spontaneously rebooting itself. This is where the Refers to and Referred to by relationships come into play—the email ticket would reference the earlier ticket. These relationships are bi-directional: when ticket A has a referred to relationship with ticket B, ticket B necessarily has a referred to by relationship with ticket A. RT maintains these relationships automatically, although it doesn't try to discover them for you. Figure 3-11 shows the *Refers to* relationship in the Links box on the main ticket page.

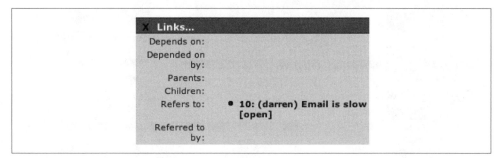

Figure 3-11. Refers to relationship

Searching for Tickets

In an active RT instance, with thousands of tickets, finding the ones you are interested in can quickly become a chore. Luckily, all of the ticket metadata we've been harping about is searchable. To start a new search, click on the *Tickets* link in the main menu. This takes you to an empty ticket search form, as shown in Figure 3-12, a very flexible and powerful search tool.

The Add Criteria section is less complicated than it looks. Each criterion you want to add is represented by a row of form elements. For example, the selected options in Figure 3-13 search for tickets where the queue is **General**, the status is **open**, the owner is **Nobody**, and the priority is greater than **90**.

When you click the *Add* button, it adds all the criteria in Figure 3-13 to the query at once. The next screen clears the Add Criteria section, but it lists the criteria in the Query section toward the upper right of the page, as shown in Figure 3-14.

The query builder also allows you to choose the fields you want to display when listing your search results. The default display shows many fields, but you can limit the display to only those fields you want in the Display Columns box at the bottom of the search form page, shown in Figure 3-15.

Under Show Columns you can remove unwanted fields from the display or move a field forward "^" or back "^" in the display order. Under Add Columns you can

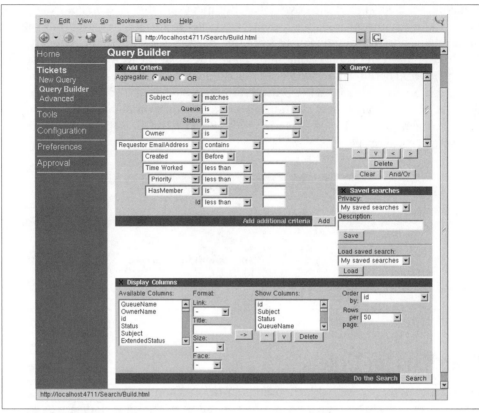

Figure 3-12. Search form

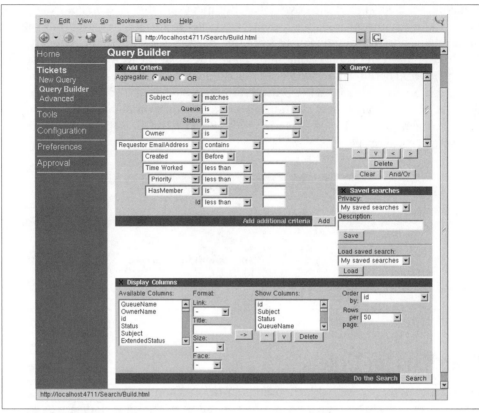

Figure 3-13. Search for tickets

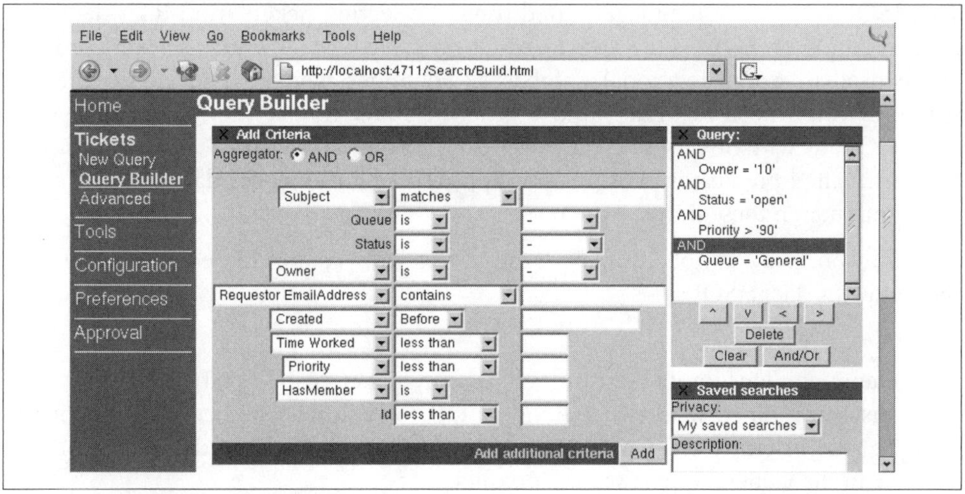

Figure 3-14. Constructed query

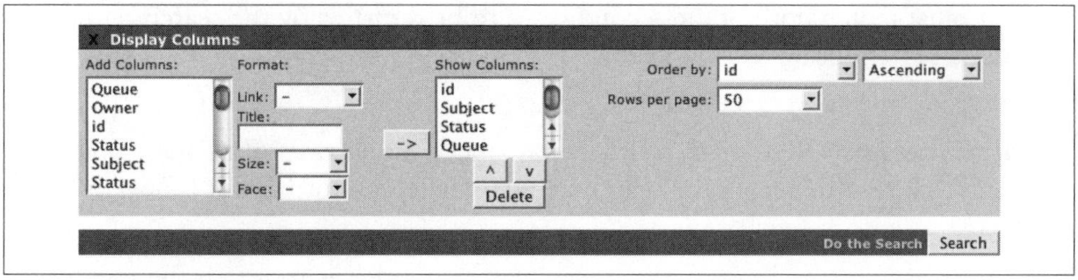

Figure 3-15. Display Columns

select a new column to add to the display, set a link target, title text, and text style for it under Format, then add it to the display with the "->" button. At Order by, select which column to sort the results and whether to sort them ascending or descending. At Rows per page, select how many results to display at a time.

Once you've created your query and chosen the fields you want to display, execute the search by clicking the Search button at the bottom of the form.

Understanding TicketSQL

Ticket searches in RT use a special-purpose query language called *TicketSQL*. The graphical query builder above generates TicketSQL for the search you want to perform. The Advanced link in the Tickets menu lets you write your own TicketSQL query from scratch.

If you generate a query with the query builder, and then click Advanced, the text area will be populated with your query. This is useful for learning TicketSQL.

TicketSQL is a simple language geared toward selecting tickets from RT's database. It's a variation on SQL — the *Structured Query Language* — which is a standard language used to query relational databases. To understand how to create effective searches, you'll need to understand a little bit about how TicketSQL works. With TicketSQL, as with SQL, you create a series of zero or more name = value conditions (they are called predicates in SQL), and apply these limits to the data set. The set of items that match these limits is the result.

Here is a concrete example: to find all the tickets with a status of new, you would use the following TicketSQL:

```
status = 'new'
```

Simple enough. This limits the result set to only tickets with a status of new. Multiple clauses are joined with either *AND* or *OR* to indicate whether both conditions must be true or either one can be true. A search for all tickets with a status of new that live in the General queue would look like:

```
status = 'new' AND queue = 'General'
```

A ticket must match both of these conditions to be returned by the search. However, consider a search for tickets with a status of either new or open:

```
status = 'new' OR status = 'open'
```

This time, because OR is used, a ticket may match either one of the two conditions in order to be returned from the search. A ticket will be returned if it is new or if it is open.

You can have as many limits as you want. Use parentheses to group the conditions whenever they get a little hairy. Here is a search for tickets in either the General or Customer Support queues with a status of new or open that are owned by the user *aml*:

```
(status = 'new' OR status = 'open')
AND
(queue = 'General' OR queue = 'Customer Support')
AND
owner = 'aml'
```

You can search for custom field values in the same way as standard ticket attributes.[*] Simply prefix the name of the custom field with CF. to indicate to the TicketSQL parser that you are searching over a custom field:

```
(status = 'open' OR status = 'new')
AND CF.Visibility != 'private'
```

---

[*] See "CustomFields" in Chapter 8 and the examples in Chapter 7 for more on custom fields.

Downloading Search Results

From the search results page, you have several display options. The most obvious is to choose the specific ticket you were looking for, and display that one. However, there are times when you might want to manipulate the tickets in an external program, so RT defines the standard export formats spreadsheet and RSS. The links to these exports are in the lower right corner of the search results page.

The RSS version of the search is useful for maintaining a list of tickets in a format usable by an RSS aggregator.* The spreadsheet version is really tab-separated values that most spreadsheet programs—Excel or Gnumeric, for example—can import. Many of these programs can be configured to retrieve results directly from the web, which may be even more convenient.

Updating Many Tickets at Once

Sometimes, you need to perform the same operation on a bunch of tickets at once. For example, when an employee leaves, you might need to reassign all of his tickets to someone else. Whenever a search returns multiple tickets, you can use the bulk update form to modify all of them. The lower right of the search results page has a link titled Update multiple tickets. This brings you to a new form, shown in Figure 3-16.

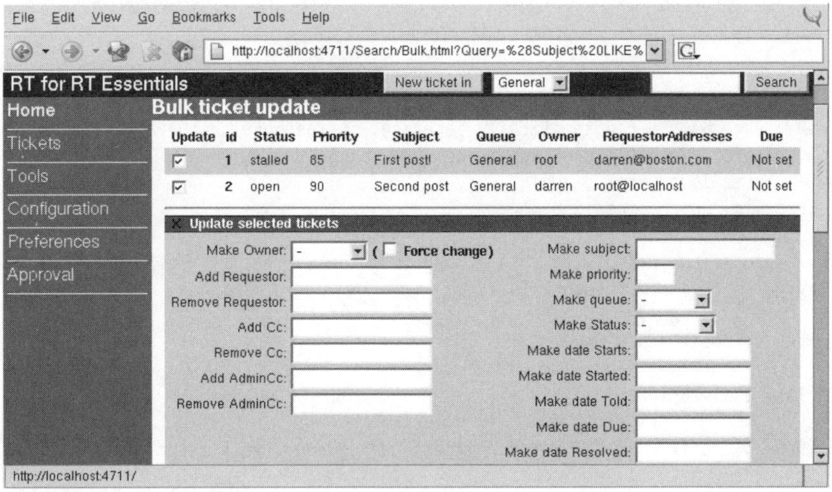

Figure 3-16. Bulk ticket update

This form has many of the same sections as the Jumbo form, and any changes you make here apply to all the selected tickets. By default, all tickets that match the

---

* RSS is a simple XML format designed for syndicating content.

search are selected, but you can exclude tickets from the bulk update by unchecking
their Update checkbox on the ticket list at the top of the form.

Email Interface

The earliest versions of RT worked almost exclusively by email, and it is still possible to interact with RT almost entirely by email. By default, RT has scrips that send
mail when interesting things happen. Whenever correspondence comes in for a
ticket, that correspondence is sent to each Watcher by email. This behavior is controlled by a scrip that can be disabled or extended by the RT administrator. Simply
responding to this email will record the response in RT, attached to the same ticket.
This makes it easy to stay in the conversation about a ticket without having to continually go back to the browser. This also allows people external to the organization
to access RT, without the need to open holes in the corporate firewall.

The mail administrator can set up specific email aliases for creating tickets.[*] By sending an email to such an alias, you create a ticket directly in RT. Such email aliases can
be very convenient for non-interactive processes that know how to send mail, such as
cron, or as destinations for web forms. Many users also find it easier to create tickets
by mail, especially when they are outside the corporate firewall.

The format of the messages that RT sends out is completely customizable by the RT
administrator and varies based on the type of transaction. For example, when you
create a new ticket, the default message looks like this:

```
Greetings,

This message has been automatically generated in response to the
creation of a trouble ticket regarding:
"My frobnitz is broken... again",
a summary of which appears below.

There is no need to reply to this message right now. Your ticket has been
assigned an ID of [RT Essentials #5].

Please include the string:

[RT Essentials #5]

in the subject line of all future correspondence about this issue. To do so,
you may reply to this message.

Thank you,


---------------------------------------------------------------------------
```

[*] The process is covered in "Configuring Inbound Email" in Chapter 2.

> My frobnitz appears to be broken again. This is the third time
> this week, is there something that can be done about this? Thanks!

Mail triggered by correspondence looks slightly different, and it contains information about the ticket and about the type of action that was taken.

To add correspondence to a ticket, reply to one of the messages that RT sends out. Your response will be recorded automatically as part of the ticket history and possibly remailed out to the other watchers, depending on how RT is configured.

Out of the box, RT limits what can be done by email, since reliably establishing identity with email is difficult and generally involves using cryptography (with PGP or S/MIME certificates). Most organizations don't have the necessary infrastructure for this, so ticket attribute changes are not allowed via email. Enhanced versions of the RT mail gateway that allow attribute changes are available as add-ons to RT.

## CHAPTER 4

Command-Line Interface

RT 2.0 included a basic command-line interface (CLI), which was simply a Perl script. It was mostly feature complete but wasn't heavily used. Because it operated independently of an RT server, it had to load all of the RT libraries before it could execute. This made it slow and tough to use interactively. It also was difficult to install, since any machine that ran it needed to have the full compliment of Perl modules, access to the database machine that was running RT, and the ability to read RT's configuration file, which includes sensitive information like the password for the database.

For RT 3.0, however, the CLI was rewritten from the ground up to be simple, lightweight, and well-suited for automated use. Instead of loading all of RT for each invocation, it does its work with an RT server over the Web. Furthermore, the API that the CLI uses to communicate with an RT server is well-documented and available for any client, written in any language. The CLI can run on any machine with Perl installed, and it doesn't require RT itself to be installed. All it requires is a network connection.

RT's CLI, generally installed as *rt*, can query the database, look at tickets or users, and even edit their contents. Although you can use *rt* from the command line in a shell session, it is also suited to being used from another program. This chapter explains how to set *rt* up, how to integrate it into your particular environment, and how to use it in a number of different scenarios.

Running the CLI

Your RT web server must be up and running for *rt* to respond in any meaningful way, even via the CLI. *rt* doesn't talk to the database directly. Instead it formulates an HTTP request and sends it to the RT server. The server then replies with the appropriate data and the CLI interprets it for you, including handling interactive forms. So, before you can use the CLI, you need to have a complete RT installation and an operational RT server. Chapter 2 covers installation. Here we assume your RT server is fully functional and running.

Make sure *rt* is in your path. It's usually located in the *bin/* directory of the main RT installation directory—*/opt/rt3*, */usr/local/rt3* or some custom location. Run *rt* without any options. It displays a help message:

```
$ rt

This is a command-line interface to RT 3.
...
```

Next, you need to configure *rt* so it can connect to the RT server. It needs two pieces of information: the URL of the server and the authentication information to use for that server. You can set this information using environment variables or in a configuration file.

The relevant environment variables are RTUSER and RTSERVER. The following example sets these in the bash shell:

```
$ export RTUSER=jdoe
$ export RTSERVER=https://rt.example.com
```

The relevant options in a configuration file are user and server. The following example shows the contents of *.rtrc* in the home directory of user jdoe:

```
user      jdoe
server    https://rt.example.com
```

If neither $RTUSER or user are defined, *rt* defaults to the current login name. For complete details on configuring the rt command-line, see Appendix C.

Most *rt* commands look something like this:

```
$rt /<action>/<options>
```

A list of available actions is available in Appendix B.

The first time you run *rt* with an action, it will prompt you for your password:

```
$ rt list "status='new'"
Password:
```

Just like in the browser, once you've entered your password, a session is established so you don't need to keep entering your password. *rt* remembers this session information by storing it in a file in your home directory: *~/.rt_sessions*, accessible only to yourself. You should protect this file with strict permissions, otherwise another user could copy it and operate on the RT server as you.

To log out from RT and end this session, use the logout command:

```
$ rt logout
```

The CLI has two different forms, a command-line tool and an interactive shell. The *rt* command is designed to be easy to use from another program or on-the-fly. The following example uses the command-line tool to tell RT to display several specific fields from the ticket with the unique id of 42.

```
$ rt show -t ticket 42 -f id,subject,status
id: ticket/42
Subject: A special number
Status: open
$
```

The interactive shell starts when you run *rt* with the action shell. In the following example, the rt> prompt remains after the command has been executed, because the RT shell is still active. This dispenses with the delay of waiting for a new shell process to startup on each invocation. The functionality is identical.

```
$ rt shell
rt> edit ticket/42 set queue=emergency status=resolved
Ticket 42 Resolved.
rt>
```

These few examples just scratch the surface of what you can do with *rt*. The rest of this chapter covers a broad range of possibilities, and Appendix B provides a quick reference to *rt*'s actions and the options for each.

Creating a Ticket

In order to create a ticket with *rt*, use the create action. This action creates users and queues in addition to new tickets, so create requires an object type:

```
$ rt create -t ticket
```

When this command is issued, your editor will open up with some basic data and fields for you to fill out:

```
# Required: Queue, Requestor, Subject

id: ticket/new
Queue: General
Requestor: jdoe
Subject:
Cc:
AdminCc:
Owner:
Status: new
Priority: 50
InitialPriority: 50
FinalPriority: 0
TimeEstimated: 0
Starts: 2004-09-21 01:05:11
Due: 2004-09-21 01:05:11
Text:
```

Once you fill in the required fields—queue, requestor, and subject—and write the file to submit the data to the server, you will get a message indicating success:

```
# Ticket 23 created.
```

If any of the required fields are not present, *rt* will reopen your editor with the data and a message indicating which fields were missing.

You also can create a ticket by passing values for the fields directly on the command line. At a minimum, you need a valid subject line and a queue:

```
$ rt create -t ticket set subject="urgent contact request" set queue=general
# Ticket 45 created.
```

Now use the show action to check that the ticket was correctly created.

```
$ rt show ticket/45 -f id,subject,queue
id: ticket/45
Subject: urgent contact request
Queue: General
```

You also can create users with the same create action, setting the minimal required name to avoid the interactive form.

```
$ rt create -t user set name=bigboote
# User 66 created.

$ rt show user/66
id: user/66
Name: bigboote
Password: ********
EmailAddress:
```

Finding a Ticket

The show action displays a ticket and its metadata, history, and attachments:

```
$ rt show ticket/3
id: ticket/3
Queue: General
Owner: darren
Creator: root
Subject: Bring more coffee rolls!
Status: open
Priority: 90
InitialPriority: 0
FinalPriority: 0
Requestors:
Cc:
AdminCc:
Created: Mon May 03 21:18:30 2004
Starts: Mon May 03 21:17:43 2004
Started: Mon May 03 22:20:23 2004
Due: Mon May 03 21:17:43 2004
Resolved: Not set
```

```
Told: Not set
TimeEstimated: 0
TimeWorked: 0
TimeLeft: 0
```

As you can see, show displays a lot of information by default. To limit the amount of detail returned, pass the -f option to specify the fields you want to see. The field names correspond to what show displays, except they are not case-sensitive. The following example limits the display to ticket ID, queue name, subject, status, and priority:

```
$ rt show ticket/3 -f id,queue,subject,status,priority
id: ticket/3
Queue: General
Subject: Bring more coffee rolls!
Status: open
Priority: 90
```

By default, show shows the object's metadata. However, there are other object attributes you might want to see, like a ticket's history or attachments. These attributes are addressed using the object specification syntax. To access the history attribute of ticket 9, use ticket/9/history.

```
$ rt show ticket/9/history
# 6/6 (/total)

63: Ticket created by jdoe
64: Cc root@localhost added by jdoe
72: Cc root@eruditorum.org added by jdoe
73: Cc root@localhost removed by root
74: Priority changed from 0 to 99 by jdoe
75: Status changed from new to open by jdoe
```

You also can display all of the attachments for a ticket with the attachments attribute:

```
$ rt show ticket/9/attachments

Attachments: 7:  (multipart/mixed / 0b), 8:  (text/plain / 29b),
             9:  (multipart/mixed / 0b), 10:  (text/plain / 0b),
             11: output.txt (text/plain / 164b),
             12:  (text/plain / 622b)
```

To view the plain-text content of one of the attachments, use the content attribute together with the attachments attribute:

```
$ rt show ticket/9/attachments/11/content

This is the output I get when I try the first solution:
...
```

Here's a command to look at the information that makes up an RT user, reducing the output by specifying certain fields only:

```
$ rt show -t user -f id,name,emailaddress,comments root
```

```
id: user/12
Name: root
EmailAddress: root@localhost
Comments: SuperUser
```

When looking at several tickets at once, note that you can specify multiple IDs separated by commas, and a range of IDs defined with a dash between the minimum and maximum ID, as in the following example:

```
$ rt show ticket/1,5-8,42 -f id,subject,status

id: ticket/1
Subject: a new ticket
Status: new

--

id: ticket/5
Subject: a new ticket
Status: new

--

id: ticket/6
Subject: a new ticket
Status: new

...
```

In addition to the type/id form, you also can specify multiple object IDs at the end of the command, separated by either spaces or commas:

```
$ rt show -t ticket -f id,subject,status 1 5-8 42

id: ticket/1
Subject: a new ticket
Status: new


--

id: ticket/5
Subject: a new ticket
Status: new


--

id: ticket/6
Subject: a new ticket
Status: new


--

id: ticket/7
Subject: a new ticket
Status: new


--

id: ticket/8
Subject: a new ticket
Status: new


--

id: ticket/42
Subject: a new ticket
Status: new
```

Replying to a Ticket

The correspond and comment actions post a response or comment to a ticket from the command line:

```
$ rt correspond -m "The vendor is supplying a patch" ticket/15
```

The -m option allows you to provide the text of the message on the command line. If this is not supplied, then *rt* will open your editor for you to enter a full message.

You also can attach files to a ticket with the -a option:

```
$ rt comment -m "This is what I see" -a screenshot.png ticket/15
```

The -w option lets you set a TimeWorked value for this comment:

```
$ rt correspond -m "Does the attached patch solve the problem?" \
> -a hairy.patch -w 300 ticket/42
```

The -c and -b options set the Cc and Bcc fields:

```
$ rt correspond -m "I'll look into this problem tonight" \
> -c root@eruditorum.org,jdoe@example.org \
> -b me@isp.net ticket/23
```

Editing a Ticket

The edit action edits object metadata. When you invoke edit with an object specification, if no additional information is given on the command line, *rt* enters interactive mode in the editor specified by the $EDITOR environment variable. When you
quit the editor, the ticket is updated. This is similar to the create action, except that
the editor displays the current values of all the fields instead of an empty template.
Only values that actually change are sent back to the server.

```
$ rt edit ticket/47

id: ticket/47
Queue: General
Owner: Nobody
Creator: jdoe
Subject: There is a light that never goes out
Status: new
Priority: 50
InitialPriority: 50
FinalPriority: 0
Requestors:
Cc:
AdminCc:
Created: Mon Sep 20 21:07:39 2004
Starts: Mon Sep 20 21:05:11 2004
Started: Not set
Due: Mon Sep 20 21:05:11 2004
Resolved: Not set
Told: Not set
TimeEstimated: 0
TimeWorked: 0
TimeLeft: 0
```

In addition, you can set many of the fields of an object using the set, add, or del subactions on the command line:

```
$ rt edit ticket/42
> add cc=root@eruditorum.org \
> del cc=root@localhost \
> set priority=99 \
> set status=open \
```

The available fields that you can set, add, or del are the same as the fields presented
when you edit an object in a text editor. Some of these attributes cannot be changed,
like Created and id.

Using the example of the user created above, modify the information by setting the emailaddress. The information in this case is sufficient to avoid entering interactive mode.

```
$ rt edit user/bigboote set emailaddress=bigboote@example.com
# User 66 updated.
```

Now use show to display the modified information.

```
$ rt show user/66 -f id,name,emailaddress
id: user/66
Name: bigboote
EmailAddress: bigboote@example.com
```

You escalate a ticket by increasing its priority:

```
$ rt edit ticket/42 set priority=80
```

To assign a ticket set the owner of the ticket. To take a ticket, set the owner to yourself.

```
$ rt edit ticket/7 set owner=fayewong
```

To resolve a ticket set the status to resolved:

```
$ rt edit ticket/15 set status='resolved'
```

Searching for Tickets

Searching with *rt* involves the list action and TicketSQL. See "Understanding TicketSQL" in Chapter 3 for an introduction to TicketSQL syntax. The command-line interface doesn't provide a query builder to help you out. The following command shows all tickets with a status of new:

```
$ rt list "status = 'new'"
3: Bring more coffee rolls!
```

The -l option to list provides a long listing, exactly the same as using the show action (see "Finding a Ticket," earlier in this chapter). The -i option only lists object identifiers:

```
$ rt list -i "status = 'new'"
ticket/3
```

rt passes your TicketSQL query directly to the RT server, which executes the query on your behalf and returns the results for *rt* to display. You can write arbitrarily complex TicketSQL, just be sure to enclose your entire query within quotes. The following example searches for open tickets in the General queue:

```
$ rt list "queue = 'General' AND status = 'open'"
3: Bring more coffee rolls!
5: My frobnitz is broken... again
```

If you double-quote the TicketSQL string, most shells will perform variable interpolation, which can be useful. For example, to get your own open tickets (assuming

your system login is the same as your RT login), you could use the $USER environ-
ment variable:

```
$ rt list "status = 'open' AND owner = '$USER'"
5: My frobnitz is broken... again
```

Here is an example of the list action, requesting a short list of all tickets which have
non-closed Status.

```
$ rt list -s -t ticket "Status != 'closed'"

1: a new ticket
21: A request subject line
42: A special number
...
```

Another, more useful example shows the LIKE query string for approximate matches.
The following example also uses the -o option to order the output based on the
status field rather than the default id.

```
$ rt list -s -o +status "status != 'closed' \
> AND subject LIKE 'request'"

21: A request subject line
...
```

The following example uses the -i switch to return only object-ids from the list
action. You can feed these results directly into another *rt* action such as show or edit,
which in turn uses the - switch to take the object-ids from STDIN. The following
example searches for a list of tickets that aren't closed and shows details for each.

```
$ rt list -i "Status != 'closed'" | rt show -

id: ticket/1
Queue: General
Owner: Nobody
Creator: root
...

--

id: ticket/42
Queue: General
Owner: Nobody
Creator: root
...
```

You can use the same strategy to update multiple tickets at the same time, for example, to add a cc address to all tickets with "urgent" in the subject:

```
$ rt list -i "Subject LIKE 'urgent'" | rt edit - add cc=bigboote@example.com
# Ticket 45 updated.
# Ticket 44 updated.
...
```

Command-Line Help

If you are ever uncertain about the syntax or options for a particular action, *rt* has a help menu. Even before the CLI is properly configured, you can view the help menu to find out which options are supported and how to use the program in the first place. To display the built-in help, either run *rt* without any arguments at all, or pass it the help parameter. Both print out a short helpful message to get you started.

```
$ rt help

This is a command-line interface to RT 3.

It allows you to interact with an RT server over HTTP, and offers an
interface to RT's functionality that is better-suited to automation
and integration with other tools.

In general, each invocation of this program should specify an action
to perform on one or more objects, and any other arguments required
to complete the desired action.

For more information:

        - rt help actions      (a list of possible actions)
        - rt help objects      (how to specify objects)
        - rt help usage        (syntax information)

        - rt help config       (configuration details)
        - rt help examples     (a few useful examples)
        - rt help topics       (a list of help topics)
```

The help output gives you information about using the help system. You can almost always go a little deeper to get the information or examples you need. You don't even need an operational RT server to access the help features—the functionality is built into the client. The help system is somewhat flexible in spelling: whether you say rt help ticket or rt help tickets is irrelevant.

```
$ rt help actions

You can currently perform the following actions on all objects:
...
```

The Shell

The *rt* command-line tool supports a shell mode, which launches an interactive shell for running actions. The primary advantage is that you don't have to wait for the client to start up on each command—it's already running and waiting for your input. To enter the shell, give the shell action to *rt*.

```
$ rt shell
rt>
```

The syntax and options for actions in the shell are the same as on the command line, except you skip the initial rt. You display a ticket with show:

```
rt> show ticket/42 -f id,queue,subject,status,priority
id: ticket/42
Queue: General
Subject: A special number
Status: open
Priority: 90
rt>
```

modify it with edit:

```
rt> edit ticket/42 set priority=80
# Ticket 42 updated.
rt>
```

and check your work with show again:

```
rt> show ticket/42 -f id,subject,priority
id: ticket/42
Subject: A special number
Priority: 80
rt>
```

Quit the RT shell session by typing ^C (Control-C).

Scripting RT

Sometimes the CLI can be overly verbose or confusing, with the many options and commands available. One way to make the interaction a bit simpler is to use your shell to simplify common operations.

Shell Functions

If you're using a Bourne-like shell (*bash*, *ksh*, */bin/sh* on most systems), you can create shell functions by placing the following in your *.profile*:

```
rtspam( ) {
  rt edit ticket/$1 set queue=spam status=deleted
}

rtresolve( ) {
  rt edit ticket/$1 set status=resolved
}

rtshow( ) {
  rt show ticket/$1
}
```

Now to use these functions directly from your shell:

```
$ rtresolve 12345
Ticket 12345 Resolved.
```

You could do this just as well with shell scripts, but shell functions are more elegant.

Shell Aliases

An alternative to dedicating a function to the task would be to do the same thing but use an *alias* instead. In a Bourne-like shell (*bash*, *ksh*, *sh*, etc.), alias commands like these may be useful in your *.profile*:

```
alias rtspam='rt edit ticket/$1 set queue=spam status=deleted'

alias rttop='rt ls -i "priority > 70 and status != resolved" | rt show - -f
id,subject'
```

If you're using a C shell (*csh* or *tcsh*), try these in your *.cshrc*:

```
alias rtspam 'rt edit ticket/\!:1 set queue=spam status=deleted'

alias rtresolve 'rt edit ticket/\!:1 set status=resolved'

alias rtshow 'rt show ticket/\!:1'
```

MIME

One useful tidbit if you're scripting RT from Perl is that the output of `rt show` is a valid MIME object. Modules like `MIME::Parser` or `Email::Simple` can parse it and manipulate it further:

```
use Email::Simple;

my $tno = $ARGV[0];
my $ticket = `rt show ticket/$tno`;
my $tobj = Email::Simple->new($ticket);

print "Ticket $tno was requested by ", $tobj->header("requestors"),
      " on ", $tobj->header("created"), ".\n";
```

## CHAPTER 5

Administrative Tasks

Day-to-day administration of an RT instance is pretty minimal. Other than the initial installation, setup, and occasional configuration tweaks, administration generally falls under a few basic areas: creating new users, modifying existing users, and backups.

Now that you have an RT server running, it's time to configure and customize it for your organization. Chapter 7 shows some example configurations, but for now, we'll help you get up to speed with a basic RT configuration.

First, you'll need to create a few users. Once that's taken care of, you'll create a queue for your project and grant your users rights to work with that queue.

Creating and Updating Users

Every person that interacts with RT has a corresponding user object. This object is loaded when the person accesses RT, whether through the web, email, or *rt*.

To create a new user, load up RT's web interface and click on *Configuration*, *Users*, and then *New user*. Figure 5-1 shows the new user page. To update an existing user (for example, one that RT created automatically from an incoming email), click *Configuration*, *Users*, and then search for the user's email address, names, or user id.

The only required attribute is *Name*, which RT uses as the username. If you want RT to be able to send email to your users, it's worth filling in the *Email Address* and *Real Name* fields. If your users will be logging into RT, you also should fill in the *Password* field.

Privileged users have access to RT's full web interface and can be granted rights directly. Unprivileged users only get access to RT's self-service interface. As of RT 3.4.2, only privileged users can be added as group member in RT, but that will change in the future.

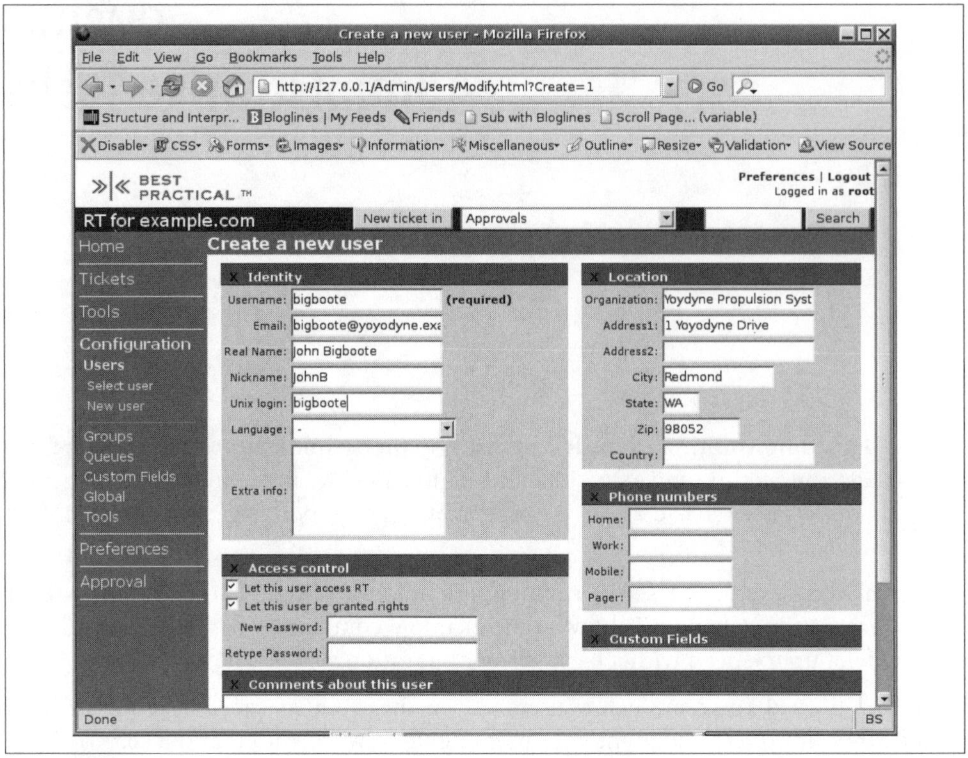

Figure 5-1. Create a new user

When RT creates a user, it creates an unprivileged user by default. To make your user privileged, check the box *Let this user be granted rights*.

If you ever need to cut off someone's access to RT, uncheck the box *Let this user access RT*. This will make sure the user can't log in to RT, but it does not fully delete the user. RT won't let you delete users because that would erase everything that user had done, and a large part of the point of a system like RT is that you don't lose history like that.

Groups

RT has a built-in group management system to make it easy to manage your users' rights and responsibilities. You can grant rights to groups and make them queue and ticket watchers. Using RT's *Saved search* system, it's also possible to let group members share saved searches among themselves. You're not required to use groups when managing RT. But it's a lot easier to pop somebody into a group when they join your team and yank them out if they leave than go through 10 different queues looking to see if you've properly yanked any rights they once had.

Creating and Updating Groups

To create, update, and disable groups, you need to be logged in to RT as a user with the AdminGroups right (or SuperUser). The first step is to go to the group management interface. From RT's web interface, click *Configuration*, then *Groups*, then *New group*. You should now be on RT's new group page, shown in Figure 5-2.

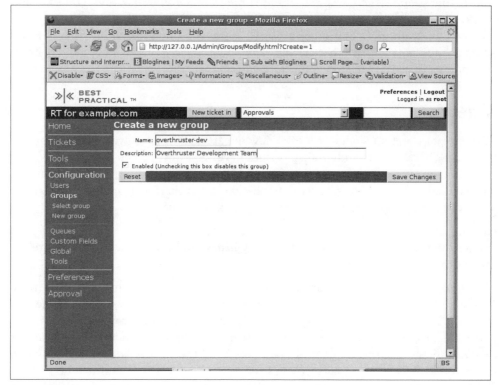

Figure 5-2. Create a new group

Enter a name and description for your group. The name will be seen primarily by people, not by computers, so make sure it's easy to understand when you (or somebody else) come back to it in six months. "Staff," "IT Department," and "Nuclear Weapons Development Team" are all fine names. *Description* is strictly optional and is just another place for you to record a bit more data about what this group is for.

Disabling a Group

As with many other things in RT, you can't ever delete a group, since you'd lose historical information about what happened to that group. You can, however, disable groups, by unchecking the *enabled* checkbox. Once the nuclear weapons project is over and the development team has retired to a small tropical island, it's safe to uncheck the *enabled* box on the group overview page for the "Nuclear Weapons Development Team."

Changing Group Membership

Once you've created a group, you can add and remove group members by navigating to the group overview page—*Configuration → Groups → <your group>*—and clicking on *Members*. Since RT 3.0, group membership has been recursive—groups can contain both users and other groups. There isn't any limit to how many levels deep groups can contain other groups. The only thing a group can't contain is itself, but don't worry, RT will stop you before you do that.

Queues

You'll want to set up a queue for each new department or long-lived project that you track in RT. Like users and groups, queues never go away, so you don't want to create too many. Create a queue each time you have a set of tasks or requests that will be handled by a separate group of people who track their own special metadata or have different privacy requirements than your existing queues.

If you've been following along, the instructions for creating a queue are going to look rather familiar. Click *Configuration*, then *Queues*, and then *New queue*. Figure 5-3 shows the new queue page.

The *Queue Name* is the primary way that you'll see the queue in the web interface and also from the mail gateway and some scrips. While you can use any name you want, it's easiest to stick with names that don't contain apostrophes, slashes, and other characters that might need special escaping. The *Reply Address* and *Comment Address* fields determine what RT will stick in the return address of outgoing response and comment emails. If you leave them blank, they default to the system-wide settings in your configuration file. RT also lets you set a default initial priority for tickets in the queue, as well as a final priority that only kicks in if you use the RT escalation tool.* If you fill in the *Requests should be due in __ days* field, RT will automatically assign a due date that many days in the future for your tickets.

Don't forget to set up RT's incoming mail gateway for your new queues. See Chapter 2 for instructions on how to do that.

---

* Run perldoc /opt/rt3/bin/rt-crontool for more information about the escalation tool.

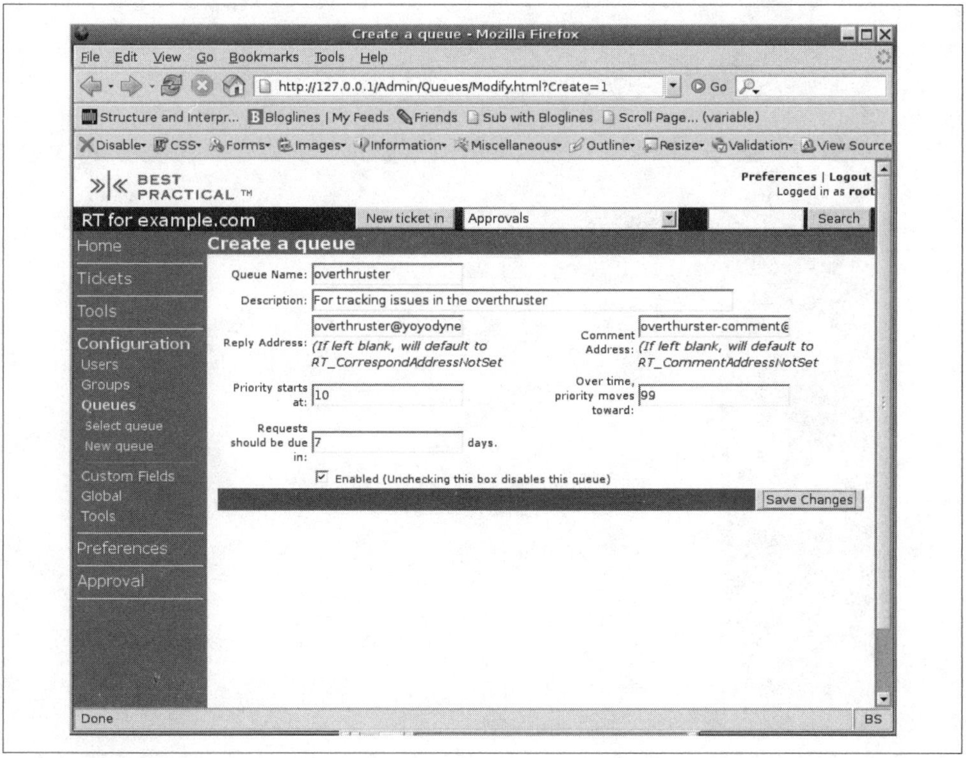

Figure 5-3. Create a new queue

Roles

Once you've created a new queue, you should set up the default Cc and AdminCc lists for it. From the queue overview page (*Configuration → Queue → <your queue>*), click *Watchers*. Figure 5-4 shows the queue watchers page.

You can search for users and groups to add to the queue's Cc and AdminCc lists. These people will be added implicitly to those roles for every ticket in the queue and may also be granted rights based on your queue access control configuration.

Access Control

You can grant per-queue rights to users or to groups. We generally recommend that you grant all rights to roles and groups, as it makes administration much easier. From the queue overview page (*Configuration → Queue → <your queue>*), click *Group Rights*. On this page, shown in Figure 5-5, you can grant rights to role groups such as Requestor, AdminCc, and Cc, as well as system-internal groups like Everyone and Privileged.

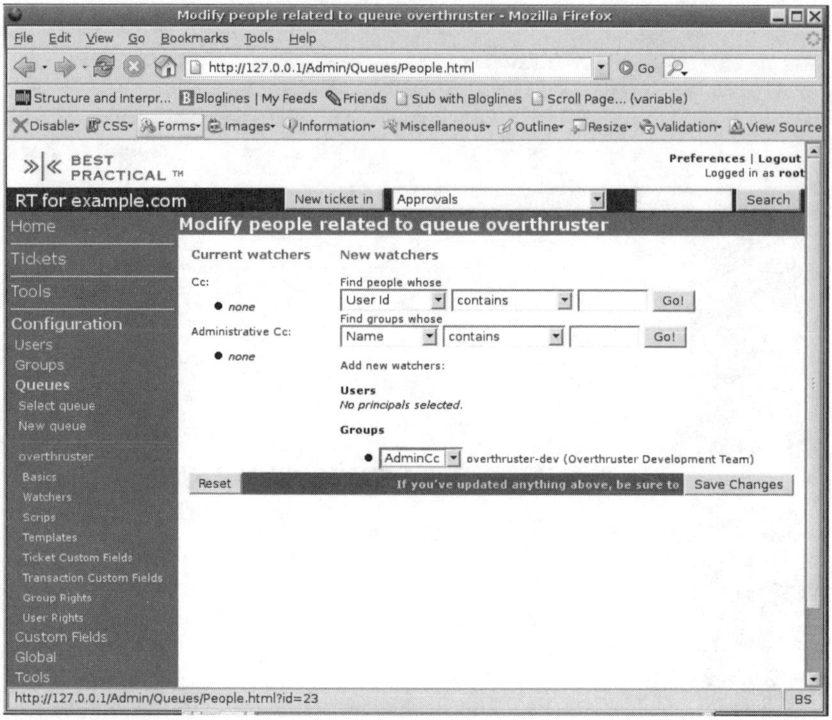

Figure 5-4. Queue watchers

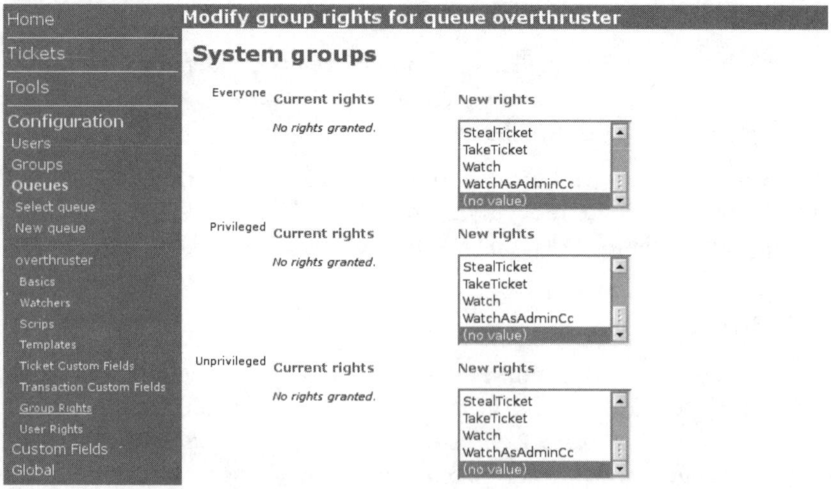

Figure 5-5. Granting group rights to a queue

To allow arbitrary remote users to submit tickets into a given queue by email, grant the system-internal group Everyone the rights SeeQueue, CreateTicket, ReplyToTicket, and CommentOnTicket.

To make sure your staff can work with tickets, you should grant your staff group all the following additional rights: ShowTicket, ShowTicketComments, Watch, WatchAsAdminCc, OwnTicket, and ModifyTicket. If you've given your staff group an AdminCc role for the queue, you can grant only these rights to the AdminCc role group.

If you'll be opening up the self-service interface to your requestors, you'll also need to grant the Requestor role group the ShowTicket right.

Scrips

Out of the box, RT comes with a relatively straight-forward set of scrips. These scrips take care of making sure that Requestors get an autoresponse when they create a ticket and that everyone gets copies of relevant email and other ticket updates. You can add custom scrips either globally or per queue, but they aren't required for making RT work correctly. We'll go into more detail about scrips in Chapter 6.

Custom Fields

RT lets you define custom fields that apply to tickets, ticket updates, users, or groups. People mainly use custom fields to track additional site-specific metadata. We've seen them used for simple things, such as the version number of a software package where a bug was found, and more complex things, such as whether someone enquiring about renting a vacation home needed a place that accepted pets.

As of this writing, RT supports five different sorts of custom fields: *Select* to pick from list, *Freeform* to type a line of text, *Text* to type a large block of text, *Wikitext* to hold multi-line blocks of wikitext, *Binary* to upload a file, and *Image* to upload an image. For each of these types except Text, you can pick whether you want your users to be able to enter one or many values. In the near future, we expect to add additional field types, as well as validated and mandatory fields.

Setting up Custom Fields

To create a custom field, click *Configuration* → *Custom Fields* → *New Custom field*. You'll need to fill in a Name for your field and pick which sort of field you want, as well as saying whether it applies to tickets, ticket updates (transactions), users, or groups. If you created a Select field, you can build up a list of possible values for the field after you create the field. Figure 5-6 shows the form for creating or editing a custom field with the values options for Select fields.

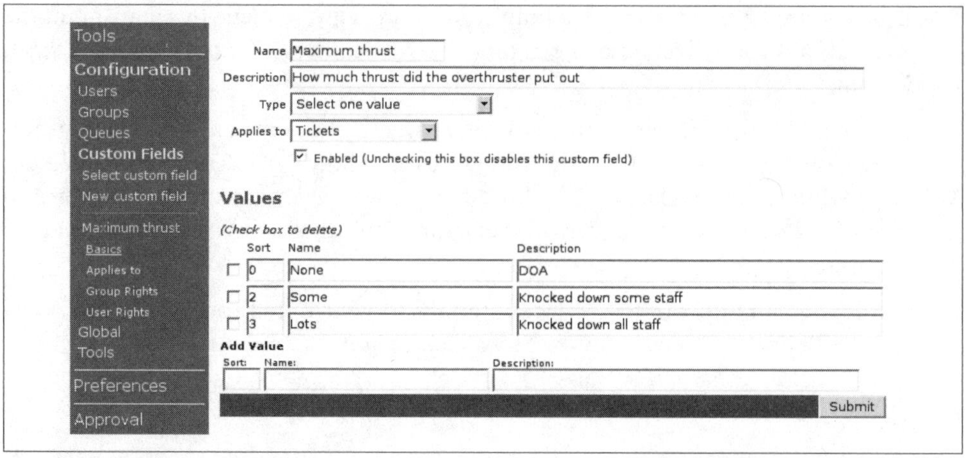

Figure 5-6. Custom fields

RT lets you switch a custom field's type, even when it's already in active use. Toggling a Image field into a Binary field is perfectly safe. It's even generally safe to turn a Select custom field into a Freeform field, since RT stores custom field values by value instead of by reference.

Access Control

Each custom field has its own access control. This means that it's easy to create fields that only certain users see, even if your tickets are otherwise public. To modify your field's access control, click *Configuration* → *Custom Fields* → *<your custom field>* → *Group Rights*. Figure 5-7 shows the custom field rights page.

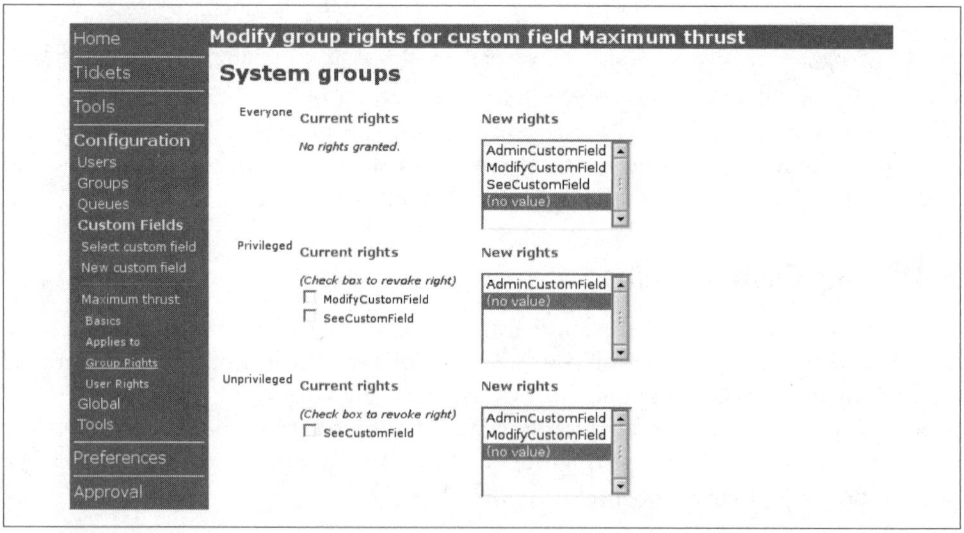

Figure 5-7. Custom field rights

The AdminCustomField right governs who can change a field's name, values, and access control. SeeCustomField determines who can see that a custom field even exists, and ModifyCustomField determines who can set a custom field's value for a particular ticket, transaction, user, or group.

Tying Custom Fields to Objects

Regular ticket custom fields apply either globally or to any set of one or more queues. To tie your new custom field to your queues, click *Configuration → Custom Fields → <your custom field> → Applies to.* From this page, you can pick one or more queues for your custom field. If you want your custom field to apply to all queues, even queues you haven't created yet, click *Configuration → Global → Custom Fields → Tickets,* and pick the fields you want to make global.

Day-to-Day Management

Most days, you won't need to think about RT management. Sometimes, you'll need to reset a user's password, add a queue, or update someone's permissions, but RT generally takes care of itself. In this section, we'll show you how to take care of a few of the most common day-to-day tasks you'll encounter.

Setup External Authentication

Some organizations invest a fair amount of time to set up a single sign-on system of one sort or another. While there are many different ways to get RT to support single sign-on, the easiest is to configure RT to let your webserver deal with authentication; most single sign-on frameworks already have a good solution for Apache authentication. If you set $WebExternalAuth to 1 in RT's configuration file, RT will trust whatever your webserver says about who is currently logged in. If the webserver tells RT that a user RT's never heard of has logged in, it's possible to have RT automatically create the user. To do this, just set $WebExternalAuto to 1.

Remove a Transaction

Sometimes, someone puts something into RT that really should never have been there in the first place, like the entire company's salary list or the CEO's baby pictures. When you absolutely need to make sure that content is purged from RT, it's possible, though not encouraged. First, find the transaction's ID. You can do this by looking at the URL for the # anchor next to the transaction. Let's say that it reads *http://rt.example.com/Ticket/Display.html?id=3700#txn-33070.* That means you want to get rid of transaction 33070.

The following code will take care of it for you:

```
perl -I/opt/rt3/lib -MRT -e '
    RT::LoadConfig(); RT::Init();
```

```
my $t = RT::Transaction->new($RT::SystemUser);
$t->Load(33070);
print $t->Delete;
'
```

Track Email Sent

RT logs information about each message it sends out, as well as each message it considers sending out. All outgoing mail about a given ticket update is sent by a scrip. Each scrip evaluates some sort of condition, such as *Is this a new ticket being created?* or *Is this a private comment?* If the answer to the question is Yes, then RT moves on to whichever action you've associated with that scrip. It might be an action such as notify the requestor or notify the owner. RT then sets up an email message using the template you've defined for the scrip and checks to make sure that it's actually being sent to someone. RT logs this process using its standard logging framework. Log messages about scrip-generated email are keyed by the outgoing message's Message-Id header. You can use that identifier to trace a message RT sends as it makes its way across the Internet from your RT server to the recipient's local email server. The example below shows an autoreply being sent out to *jesse@example.com*.

```
Jul  4 22:15:53 pallas RT: <rt-3.2.HEAD-5813-28448-22.1.5718764250061@example.com>
#5813/28448 - Scrip 22
Jul  4 22:15:53 pallas RT: <rt-3.2.HEAD-5813-28448-22.1.5718764250061@example.com>
sent To: jesse@example.com Cc:  Bcc:
```

Let's take a look at these log messages in a bit more detail. The first message gives us a heads-up that RT is considering sending some sort of email. In this case, scrip 22 sends an autoreply to the ticket's creator when a ticket is created. This scrip is acting on transaction 28448 on ticket 5813. The second message tells us that RT has sent out this email to just one person, *jesse@example.com*. If RT had decided to scrap the email, we'd see a different second message:

```
Jul  4 22:15:53 pallas RT: <rt-3.2.HEAD-5813-28448-22.1.5718764250061@example.com> No
recipients found. Not sending
```

This usually means that you have a scrip set up to notify a ticket's Owner or AdminCc or manually entered Cc or Bcc recipients, but there weren't any.

Report Failed Logins

RT reports all failed logins at the error log level. Generally, failed logins can be found in */var/log/syslog*. Depending on how you've configured the *syslog* service, errors might turn up in different places, but they'll all look something like this:

```
Jul  4 21:08:01 pallas RT: FAILED LOGIN for root from 209.6.22.246
```

You can use standard log summarizing tools to automatically extract all RT login failures from your syslog. A quick and dirty shell script to send you mail about all failed RT logins today would look something like this:

```
#!/bin/sh
grep `date +%b%e` /var/log/syslog  \
    | grep RT:\ FAILED\ LOGIN \
    | mail -s "Today's failed RT logins" rt-admin-user
```

Backing Up RT

RT doesn't store anything important about your users, groups, tickets, or queues directly on your filesystem. All the data you need to worry about on a day-to-day basis lives inside the database you've set up for RT.

Backing Up RT's Data

If you're already backing up your MySQL, PostgreSQL, or Oracle server, you can skip down to *Backing up the RT Application* below.

If you're still with us, that probably means you're one of the silent majority of users who doesn't yet backup your data, because you haven't yet suffered catastropic data-loss. Backing up RT is quick and easy. All you need to do is take a snapshot of your database and spool it out to disk as a series of SQL statements that you can run later if you need to recreate your database.

MySQL

MySQL's *mysqldump* command is a very convenient way to backup any MySQL database. It exports the contents of the database as a series of CREATE TABLE and INSERT statements, which then can be replayed to recreate a database. This method is slower than a disk-based byte-by-byte copy, but you are guaranteed to have a usable dump that can be used to recreate your database with minimal effort.

```
mysqldump --opt --add-drop-table --single-transaction \
-u rt_user -prt_pass -h databasehost rt3 > rt3-mysql-backup
```

rt_user, rt_pass, and rt_hostname should match the user, password, and hostname in your *RT_Config.pm* or *RT_SiteConfig.pm*.

PostgreSQL

pg_dump lets you dump out a live postgres database, including all schema and content. All of the previous comments about MySQL apply here, too.

```
pg_dump --clean --blobs --format=C -U rt_user rt3 > rt3-postgres-backup
```

Oracle

If you're running Oracle, it probably means you have a DBA. Take your DBA out to lunch, and discuss backing up your RT database. It's a business expense and a great way to ensure his cooperation if you ever need your RT database restored at 2 a.m.

SQLite

SQLite uses a single file as its entire database. To be sure your database is consistent, stop your RT daemon, copy the database file to your backup media, and start RT again. This should be automated with *cron*, and done regularly. SQLite's one file makes backups convenient. For example, you can use a source control system such as Subversion or CVS (in binary mode) to manage the file.

Backing Up the RT Application

The RT application itself is stored on disk. Certain cache files get written out at run-time, but they're not important to keep in the event of a catastrophe. If you've just installed RT from the source distribution and haven't customized any of the source files or web templates, you can get by without backing up the RT application. Just make sure you hang onto a copy of the original source files and reinstall RT when you need to. If you've made any changes to RT's configuration files, libraries, or web templates, you should keep backups of your RT installation. There isn't any danger to backing up RT while it's accepting tickets.

The most important file to back up is *RT_SiteConfig.pm*, since this the only file you are guaranteed to have changed. You can restore an RT instance using only *RT_SiteConfig.pm* and a database dump if needed.

When you back up the RT application and libraries, be sure that you have a backup of your webserver, database server, Perl installation, and other similar things on which RT depends. If you plan on making extensive changes to your RT instance, you should consider storing RT's libraries and document root in a local source control repository. CVS's vendor import facility was designed specifically to handle this situation (indeed, CVS originated as a way to track local modifications to vendor distributed source code), and other source control systems have analogous functionality.

Make Sure Your Backups Work!

We strongly recommend that you practice restoring your RT instance every couple of months, to make sure that your backups are working correctly and that you've got all the pieces and parts you need to get RT up and running normally after a catastrophe.

Even if you can't practice a restore very often, make sure you've done it at least once so that it's not a learning experience when you've got users breathing down your neck.

Restoring RT

The worst has happened. Your RT database server went up in a big ball of flames about 20 minutes ago. And your users are already clamoring for you to replace the server and let them get on with their work.

To get RT up and running after a crash, restore your RT application from your regular system backups. If that's not an option, start with a brand new, fresh installation of the RT version you were running. Make sure RT's configuration file has the same values it had before your crash. It's particularly important that you get the $rtname and $Organization variables right, or RT won't work properly.

Restoring RT Data

Once you have RT installed, it's time to restore your existing RT database. This is essentially the reverse of the dump process you go through when making backups.

MySQL

To restore a mysql-based RT instance, you just need to use the `mysql` command to feed your *rt3* database back in from your backups using this command:

```
mysql -u rt_user -prt_pass -h rt_hostname rt3 < rt3-mysql-backup
```

Postgres

You can restore a Postgres RT instance from a backup you made with the procedure we outlined earlier using this command:

```
pg_restore --create < rt3-postgres-backup
```

All the data postgres needs about the database name, tables, and columns is embedded in the backup file.

SQLite

Since SQLite stores its database in a single file, restoration means copying the backup file to where RT expects to find it. What could be simpler?

Oracle

Ask your DBA to switch RT over to the hot spare database they configured when setting up your Oracle instance in the first place or to restore from the most recent nightly backup.

Recover a Lost Administrative Password

RT's default administrative user is called *root*, after the Unix super-user of the same name. When you installed RT, this user started off with the default password password. If you followed our instructions, you changed this password immediately. For one reason or another, you might no longer know root's password. Either you changed it to something you couldn't possibly forget or, more likely, someone else set up your RT instance and is hiking in the Himalayas or otherwise uncontactable. No problem. Just log in as another user who has either the SuperUser right or the AdminUsers right and change root's password. If you don't happen to have one of those around, you can write a simple Perl one-liner to change a user's password. In the example below, we're going to change root's password to *secret*. You'll need to run this script as root or as another user who can read RT's private configuration file.

```
perl -I/opt/rt3/lib -MRT -e'
    RT::LoadConfig(); RT::Init();
    my $u = RT::User->new($RT::SystemUser);
    $u->Load("root");
    print $u->SetPassword("secret");
'
```

When you run the script, you should see the response "The new value has been set." Then you should be all set to log in as root.

Recover SuperUser Privileges

If you ever find yourself in the unfortunate situation of having removed your only administrator's SuperUser rights, don't panic.

The following one-liner uses the RT API and the internal module RT::SystemUser to grant the root user the SuperUser right safely. As with the last tip, you'll need to run this as a local user who can access the RT config file.

```
perl -I/opt/rt3/lib -MRT -e'
    RT::LoadConfig(); RT::Init();
    my $u = RT::User->new($RT::SystemUser);
    $u->Load("root");
    print $u->PrincipalObj->GrantRight(
        Object => $RT::System,
        Right  => "SuperUser"
    );
'
```

If you've really clobbered your administrative user or don't even know who your RT administrative user is, don't despair. This tip will turn *any* RT user into a superuser in seconds. Just replace root in this example with any other valid username.

## CHAPTER 6

Scrips

Scrips, often used together with templates, are the quickest and simplest way to customize RT's behavior. A scrip consists of a condition, an action, and a template. RT comes with a number of pre-defined conditions, actions, and templates, but you also can write your own. Scrips give you the freedom to implement whatever business logic you need.

How Scrips Work

Custom conditions and actions can be created via RT's web interface, or you can create a Perl module for each custom condition and action.

Additionally, a scrip can have custom cleanup code that will run after all other code, but before the scrip exits. Custom scrip code is always written in standard Perl, and templates are created using the `Text::Template` module.

Scrips can be applied across all queues or to individual queues. With the current version of RT, if you want to apply the same scrip to a subset of queues, you will have to go into each queue's configuration and create the scrip for each one.

The scrips system is the last major part of RT that works exactly how it did when RT 2.0 came out in 2001.

In a future version of RT, the scrips system will be overhauled to make it easier to specify which scrips apply to which queues and to build more complex workflow.

Transactions

A scrip is always run in the context of a transaction. Transactions represent a set of changes to a ticket. For example, when a ticket is resolved, its status changes, and a comment or reply may be added as part of the same transaction.

The transaction object is important when implementing custom scrip conditions and actions, as it lets you see what is being changed in the ticket.

Cc and AdminCc

Scrip action and templates often refer to Cc and AdminCc as email recipients, which are simply two generic recipient groups. The AdminCc group usually consists of some or all of the privileged RT users. The Cc group would be anyone else with an interest in a particular ticket. For example, in a tech support department, the support staff and their supervisors could all be in the AdminCc group. The AdminCc group consists of the people who work directly with RT the most. RT is by default configured to send different types of messages based on whether or not the recipient is in the AdminCc or Cc group. For example, by default RT includes the URL for a ticket when emailing a member of the AdminCc group.

Conditions

RT comes with a set of standard conditions for scrips, as shown in Table 6-1.

Table 6-1. Scrip conditions

Condition	Triggered
On Create	When a new ticket is created.
On Transaction	When a ticket is modified in any way.
On Correspond	When a reply is created for the ticket. This condition is triggered for both replies created via the web interface and for replies received via email.
On Comment	When a comment is created for the ticket. Again, this applies to both the web interface and incoming email.
On Status Change	When the ticket's status changes.
On Resolve	When the ticket is marked as resolved.
On Priority Change	When the ticket's priority changes.
On Owner Change	When the ticket's owner changes.
On Queue Change	When the ticket is moved to a new queue.

Additionally, you can create a new scrip with a user-defined action. The following example is a very simple user-defined condition:

```
$self->TicketObj->status eq 'deleted';
```

This condition is true whenever a ticket's status is changed to deleted. This code is suitable for pasting into RT's web interface.

The equivalent Perl module would look like this:

```
package RT::Condition::OnDelete;

use strict;
use base 'RT::Condition::Generic';

sub IsApplicable {
    my $self = shift;
```

```perl
        return ($self->TicketObj->status eq 'deleted');
    }

1;
```

If your RT base directory is */opt/rt3*, this code could be installed as */opt/rt3/local/lib/RT/Condition/OnDelete.pm*. You can automate this process using the Module::Install::RTx module, which is covered in Chapter 10.

You also need to make RT aware of this module, which means adding some information to the database. Mucking around with the database directly is not a good idea, but there is a simple way to write command-line scrips to manipulate RT's database.

Use the RT::Interface::CLI module to talk to RT:

```perl
#!/usr/bin/perl

use strict;
use lib "/opt/rt3/lib";

use RT;
use RT::Interface::CLI qw( CleanEnv GetCurrentUser );
use RT::ScripCondition;

CleanEnv();
RT::LoadConfig();
RT::Init();

my $user = GetCurrentUser();
unless( $user->Id ) {
    print "No RT user found. Please consult your RT administrator.\n";
    exit 1;
}
```

This first part is the voodoo needed to begin doing anything with RT from a command-line script. When GetCurrentUser() is called, it will look for a user in the RT database matching the username running the script. It does this by checking the *Unix login* field for the user, which by default is empty. So you will need to set this for at least one user via the web interface.

Now that you have RT initialized and the current user loaded, you can add the following code to make RT aware of this new condition:

```perl
my $sc = RT::ScripCondition->new($user);

$sc->Create( Name                => 'On Delete',
             Description         => 'When a ticket is deleted',
             ExecModule          => 'OnDelete',
             ApplicableTransTypes => 'Status',
           );
```

The Name is a short description for the condition and will be seen in the web interface.

After you run this script, when you go to create a new scrip in the web interface, you'll see a new condition available in the condition select list.

Later in this chapter we'll explore the possibilities for custom conditions in more detail.

Actions

An action is what the scrip does if its condition is true. RT comes with a number of actions built in, as shown in Table 6-2.

Table 6-2. Scrip actions

Action	What it does
Autoreply to Requestors	Send email to the ticket's requestors. This differs from the various "notify" actions in that the generated email's "From" header will have only the queue name.
Notify Requestors, Notify Owner, etc.	Send email to the specific group, such as the ticket's requestors, its owner, etc. The email is generated using the template associated with the scrip.
Notify Other Recipients	This action allows you to specify arbitrary recipients by setting the "To" header in the template. In the template section, we create a custom template that takes advantage of this.
Notify Owner As Comment, Notify Ccs as Comment, etc.	When a notification is sent as a comment, the reply to address will be the queue's comment address, not its correspondence address.
Create Tickets	This action can be used to create one or more new tickets based on the template associated with the scrip. This is one of the features that allows you to create workflows using RT.
Open Tickets	This action opens a ticket. RT uses this action to open resolved tickets when they receive correspondence.

Of course, just as with conditions, you can write your own custom actions. And also like conditions, these actions can be defined either through a bit of Perl code pasted into the web interface, or as a separate module.

Let's assume that you have an LDAP directory that lets you look up the department someone belongs to, based on their email address. You'd like to include that department as a custom field for all tickets.

To do that, you can create a custom action that sets this field for all newly created tickets. That means you would have this action run when the *On Create* condition was triggered, as part of the action preparation.

Your action code would look something like this:

```
my $email = ($self->TicketObj->RequestorAddresses)[0];

my $ldap = Net::LDAP->new( 'ldap.example.com' );
$ldap->bind;

my $msg = $ldap->search( base   => 'dc=ldap,dc=example,dc=com',
                         filter => "(email=$email)",
                       );

my $entry = $msg->entry(0);

my $dept = $entry->get_value('ou');

my $cf = RT::CustomField->new( $RT::SystemUser );
$cf->LoadByName( Name => 'Department' );

$self->TicketObj->AddCustomFieldValue( Field => $cf, Value => $dept );

return 1;
```

This same code as a Perl module looks like this:

```
package RT::Action::AddDepartment;

use strict;

use base 'RT::Action::Generic';

sub Prepare {
    my $self = shift;

    my $email = ($self->TicketObj->RequestorAddresses)[0];

    my $ldap = Net::LDAP->new( 'ldap.example.com' );
    $ldap->bind;

    my $msg = $ldap->search( base   => 'dc=ldap,dc=example,dc=com',
                             filter => "(email=$email)",
                           );

    my $entry = $msg->entry(0);

    my $dept = $entry->get_value('ou');

    my $cf = RT::CustomField->new( $RT::SystemUser );
    $cf->LoadByName( Name => 'Department' );

    $self->TicketObj->AddCustomFieldValue( Field => $cf, Value => $dept );

    return 1;
}

1;
```

Again, if you add a new module, you need to make RT aware of it by adding it to the database. This can be done with a script just like the one for adding new conditions, except with the following code at the end:

```
my $sc = RT::ScripAction->new($user);

$sc->Create( Name        => 'Add Department',
             Description => 'set department custom field for new tickets',
             ExecModule  => 'AddDepartment',
           );
```

After creating this action, you can use the web interface to add a new scrip with the condition set to *On Create* and the action set to *Add Department*. You also need to make sure that there is a custom field named *Department*.

Templates

Each scrip can have one associated template. These usually generate email, but they can be used for any purpose you like. They allow you to generate arbitrary text based on the content of a transaction. For example, a scrip with the *Create Tickets* action will use the output of its template to generate new tickets.

Templates are written using the Text::Template templating language, which is a very simple templating language allowing you to embed Perl in text. Perl code is placed in curly braces ({ and }). Everything else is plain text.

RT installs the base templates shown in Table 6-3.

Table 6-3. Standard templates

Template	Use
Blank	Because every scrip must have an associated template, you should use this template when you don't want to generate any text.
Autoreply	The default auto-reply template, which can be used when a new ticket is created.
Transaction	This is a very simple template that only includes some of the ticket's information such as status and subject.
Admin Correspondence	Shows the contents of the transaction along with a URL to view the ticket.
Correspondence	Simply includes the contents of the transaction.
Admin Comment	Used to send comments to admins when one is made.
Status Change	A template specifically designed for sending email to admins when a ticket's status is changed.
Resolved	This template is designed to be sent to requestors when a ticket is resolved.

You can make your own custom templates. If you're using a template to send email, you also can set the email headers from the template.

Let's assume that you created a custom scrip to fire whenever someone steals a ticket. You want to send email to the former owner letting them know this.

The following example is a template for that email:

```
To: { my $old_owner = RT::User->new( $self->CurrentUser );
      $old_owner->Load( $Transaction->OldValue );
      $old_owner->EmailAddress() }
Subject: Ticket #{ $Ticket->Id() } taken by { $Ticket->OwnerObj->Name() }

A ticket you owned:

  { $Ticket->Subject() }

has been taken by { $Ticket->OwnerObj->Name() }.

  { $RT::WebURL }Ticket/Display.html?id={ $Ticket->Id() }
```

If the template is being used to send an email, then you can set headers simply by specifying them as name/value pairs at the beginning of the template. In the code just shown the To and Subject header is set from the template.

To actually send this message only when a ticket is stolen also requires a custom condition, which we will see later.

If a transaction adds attachments to a ticket, and you want to include those attachments with the outgoing email, add this line to the top of your template:

```
RT-Attach-Message: Yes
```

Gritty Details

Now that you have seen a number of simple examples of custom scrip code, let's get into details of how these work and what objects are available for your custom code.

Tickets and Transactions

The two most important objects for custom scrip code and custom templates are the ticket and transaction objects. The ticket object is the ticket being modified. Any changes applied as part of the current transaction are reflected in the state of the related ticket object.

The transaction object represents the changes being made to the ticket. So for example, if the owner of a ticket is changed, then the transaction contains both the old and new owner IDs.

In a custom action or condition, these two objects are available via $self->TicketObj and $self->TransactionObj. You can access additional objects through those objects. For example, if you want the RT::User object representing a ticket's owner, you should use $self->TicketObj->OwnerObj. To get the ticket's queue object, use $self->TicketObj->QueueObj.

For more details, read the documentation for the RT::Ticket, RT::Ticket_Overlay, RT::Transaction, and RT::Transaction_Overlay modules.

Other Objects and Globals

Besides the ticket and transaction, several other pieces of the RT API often are useful when creating custom scrips.

$object->CurrentUser( )
> Most objects in the RT class hierarchy inherit from RT::Base, which provides a CurrentUser( ) method. This represents the user currently operating on the object. In the web interface, this is the logged-in user who is triggering the scrip.

RT::Nobody( )
> The RT::Nobody() function returns an RT::User object for the Nobody user. You can compare this user's ID to another user ID to check if that user is a real user. For example, you might have a condition that is true whenever the owner changes, as long as the previous owner wasn't Nobody. Or you might have an action that is triggered only when a ticket is assigned from a real user to Nobody.

RT::SystemUser( )
> RT::SystemUser() returns an RT::User object for RT's internal superuser, RT_ SystemUser. RT uses this user internally to do things that need to happen without access control, such as performing internal consistency checks. Generally, you shouldn't ever do anything as the system user, but it's ok to use to look at things if you want to avoid ACL checks.

$RT::Logger
> This is a Log::Dispatch object with outputs based on your RT config. You can call methods on this object like debug( ), warn( ), or error( ) to log output from your code. This is useful both for debugging as well as for logging serious errors.

Everything else
> Of course, RT is a large system with a complex API. There are many other objects that you may want to make use of, such as queues, users, or custom fields. See Chapter 9 and the documentation for the relevant modules for more details on the API.

Scrip Stage

When you create or modify a scrip via the web interface, you are given a choice of *Stage*. The three options are *TransactionCreate*, *TransactionBatch*, and *Disabled*. Disabled simply means that the scrip will never run, and it is a simple way to turn off a scrip that you may want to re-enable later.

The TransactionCreate stage is the default for all scrips, and it is what all the scrips created use when RT is installed.

By default, RT does not enable the TransactionBatch stage. To turn it on you must add this line to your *RT_SiteConfig.pm* file:

```
Set($UseTransactionBatch , 1);
```

The difference between the create and batch stages is only relevant when an action creates multiple transactions, which can happen quite easily with normal web interface usage. For example, if you use the *Jumbo* form to change the subject of a ticket and assign it to someone else, you will end up creating at least two transactions, one for the subject change and one for the owner change.

When scrips run in the create stage, they run once for *each* transaction. Generally, this isn't a problem, as the scrip's condition will be true only for one of these transactions. But for some types of scrips, this may be problematic.

When a scrip's stage is set to TranactionBatch, it will run only once, no matter how many transactions are generated. But it will have access to all of the transactions at once. We will show a specific example of why this is useful later.

Custom Conditions

Writing a custom condition is pretty simple. All your code has to do is return true or false. If it returns true, the scrip continues and executes its action. If it returns false, the scrip is done.

When you're creating your own condition modules, you should always subclass RT::Condition::Generic and then override the IsApplicable() method. This is how the default actions that ship with RT all work.

Custom Actions

Actions are actually divided into two phases, prepare and cleanup. The latter is often referred to as the commit phase in the internals.

If the action's prepare phase code returns a false value, then the scrip is discarded and the action's commit phase never runs. This allows an action to decide not to run. If your action always will be executed, you can just define code for the commit phase.

Note that stopping an action by returning false from the prepare phase is orthogonal to the scrip's condition. You can mix and match conditions and actions, so you will still want your action to return false if it cannot execute. For example, you may have an action that creates a new ticket for the ticket's owner. If the ticket's owner is "Nobody," you probably don't want to run the action.

The commit phase should be where the action does things like send email, create a new ticket, etc.

Custom Templates

When you create a custom action, you may want create a custom template to go with it. Or you might just want to change RT's templates for the standard actions.

As we mentioned earlier, templates use Text::Template for generating output. Of course, the authoritative source of information on the module is the module's documentation, but there are a few points worth noting:

- Anything enclosed in { curly braces } is Perl code. The code may contain multiple statements. The value of the last statement is used as output. If you do not want to generate output simply end the block with an empty string: `''`;. Each separate block is in a separate scope, so you cannot use lexical variables created in another block.

- Anything you append to the $OUT variable appears in the template's output:

  ```
  One and two:
  { for ( 1..2 ) {
        $OUT .= " * $_\n";
    }
    '';
  }
  ```

  This generates this text:

  ```
  One and two:
  * 1
  * 2
  ```

- If you want to add a curly brace to the output, you can escape it: \{.

Examples

The best way to understand what custom scrips can do is to look at some complete examples.

Your Ticket Was Stolen

The custom template we looked at earlier notified a user when another user stole their ticket. Let's examine that example in more detail. First, we'll implement it solely via the web interface, and then we'll reimplement it as custom modules.

From the web interface, we can create a new scrip. Let's call it *Ticket Stolen*. The condition should be set to *User Defined*. The action will be *Notify Other Recipients*. We will create a custom template to generate an email to the right recipient. If you created that template earlier, you can set the Template field to use that one now. Otherwise you can leave it empty for now.

The stage for this scrip will be TransactionCreate.

An OnSteal condition

Since there is no OnSteal condition built into RT, we need to create one.

The following code goes in the *Custom condition* text entry box:

```
my $trans = $self->TransactionObj;
return 0 unless $trans->Field eq 'Owner';
return 1 if $trans->OldValue != RT::Nobody( )->id( );
return 0;
```

The first thing we check is that the transaction to which the condition is being applied is changing the *Owner* field. If it's not, we return false. Obviously, stealing a ticket involves changing the ticket's owner.

Next, we check to make sure that the old owner is not the nobody user. If the ticket had no previous owner, then the ticket isn't being stolen. The RT::Nobody( )->id syntax is a bit of an oddity. We're calling a function called Nobody in the RT namespace. This function returns an RT::User object, upon which we call the id( ) method. If we just wrote RT::Nobody->id( ), the Perl interpreter would try to call the id( ) method on a non-existent RT::Nobody *class*.

Finally, we return false as a default. Adding this to the end of the condition code is a good practice, since it makes the default clear.

Our custom template

We are going to use the same template we saw earlier. Here it is again:

```
To: { my $old_owner = RT::User->new( $self->CurrentUser );
      $old_owner->Load( $Transaction->OldValue );
      $old_owner->EmailAddress( ) }
Subject: Ticket #{ $Ticket->Id( ) } taken by { $Ticket->OwnerObj->Name( ) }

A ticket you owned:

  { $Ticket->Subject( ) }

has been taken by {$Ticket->OwnerObj->Name( )}.

{ $RT::WebURL }Ticket/Display.html?id={ $Ticket->Id }
```

You might wonder what will happen if the old owner doesn't have an email address. The answer is nothing. If the template's To header is empty, then RT will not try to send email. Although it's not necessary, you could add a bit of action preparation code like this if you wanted:

```
my $old_owner = RT::User->new( $self->CurrentUser );
$old_owner->Load( $Transaction->OldValue );
return (defined $old_owner->EmailAddress( ));
```

Once the template is created, the Ticket Stolen scrip can use it. Once that's done, you're all set with your custom business logic.

AutoReply with a Password

When someone emails RT for the first time, RT will add them as a user to the data-base. However, by default this new user will not be able to log in to the system to view their tickets. If you want them to be able to log in, they need to have a password.

You can customize the existing AutoReply template to create a new password for them and include it in the response. For existing users, you can include their current password.

The customized template might look like this:

```
Subject: AutoReply: { $Ticket->Subject() }


Greetings,

This message has been automatically generated in response to the
creation of a trouble ticket regarding:
        "{ $Ticket->Subject() }",
a summary of which appears below.

There is no need to reply to this message right now.  Your ticket
has been assigned an ID of [{ $rtname } #{ $Ticket->Id() }].

Please include the string:

        [{ $rtname } #{ $Ticket->Id() }]

in the subject line of all future correspondence about this
issue. To do so, you may reply to this message.

You may log into the Request Tracker system to view your past and
current tickets at:

        { $RT::WebURL }

{
  if ( $Transaction->CreatorObj->id != $RT::Nobody->id
       && ! $Transaction->CreatorObj->Privileged
       && ! $Transaction->CreatorObj->HasPassword ) {

      my $user = RT::User->new( $RT::SystemUser );
      $user->Load( $Transaction->CreatorObj->Id );

      my ($stat, $password) = $user->SetRandomPassword();

      if ($stat) {
          my $username = $user->Name;

          $OUT .= "
When prompted to log in, please use the following credentials:
```

```
              Username: $username
              Password: $password
";
      } else {
          $RT::Logger->error( 'Error trying to set random password for '
                          . $user->Name . ": $password" );

          $OUT .= "
There was an error when trying to assign you a new password.
Please contact your local RT administrator at for assistance.
";
      }
  }
}
                      Thank you,
                      { $Ticket->QueueObj->CorrespondAddress() }


----------------------------------------------------------------------
{$Transaction->Content()}
```

This template is the same as the one that ships with RT, except for the section in the middle, which automatically assigns a new password to the user if they do not already have one.

Several pieces are worth noting in this template. First, there is the check to see if the user has a password:

```
unless ($Transaction->CreatorObj->id == $RT::Nobody->id
        && $Transaction->CreatorObj->Privileged
        && $Transaction->CreatorObj->HasPassword ) { ...
```

We want to make sure that we don't try to give the Nobody user a password, as this user is solely for internal use. We also do not want to auto-generate a password for privileged users, because we assume that the RT administrator manually manages these users. Finally, we need to make sure that the user doesn't already have a password.

When we call $user->SetRandomPassword( ) we check the return value. This method returns a two item list. The first is a return code indicating success (true) or failure (false). If creating the password succeeded, the second item is the new password, which we include in the email. If the password could not be created for some reason, the second item is the error message. We make sure to log this error so that the RT administrator can follow up on it later.

Emergency Pages

If you are using RT to handle a support or sysadmin center, it might be useful to send a message to a pager for certain types of requests.

Let's take a look at how to set up RT to send pages for new tickets with a subject matching /^Emergency/i, but only from 6 p.m. to 8 a.m. These could come from users or from system monitoring software.

This can be done by creating a custom condition and template. The condition checks the subject and time. The template creates the SMS message. To send email, we can use RT's existing Notify action.

```
package RT::Condition::OnAfterHoursEmergency;

use strict;
use base 'RT::Condition::Generic';

sub IsApplicable {
    my $self = shift;

    return 0 unless $self->TicketObj->Subject =~ /^Emergency/i;

    my $hour = (localtime)[2];

    return 0 unless $hour >= 18 || $hour <= 8;

    return 1;
}

1;
```

First, we check the ticket subject to make sure that it indicates an emergency. Then we check the time. This will work properly only if the server RT runs on has the correct time. If all of the checks pass, we return a true value. We also will want to make sure that this condition is checked only when creating a ticket, but that can be done when we register the condition with the system.

Now let's create our template:

```
From:    Yoyodyne RT <rt@yoyodyne.example.com>
To:      6125559912@pager.example.com
Subject: Yoyodyne RT 911

{ $Ticket->Subject() }
```

We want to keep the message short, so we use only the ticket's subject as the email body. The template can be created in the system with RT's web interface.

To add our custom condition, we need two steps. First, we need to save the code to our RT installation's local lib directory. This would be */opt/rt3/local/lib/RT/Condition/OnAfterHoursEmergency.pm* in this example.

Then we can use a script like the one we saw before to register the condition with RT:

```
#!/usr/bin/perl

use strict;
use lib "/opt/rt3/lib";

use RT;
use RT::Interface::CLI qw( CleanEnv GetCurrentUser );
use RT::ScripCondition;

CleanEnv();
RT::LoadConfig();
RT::Init();

my $user = GetCurrentUser();
unless( $user->Id ) {
    print "No RT user found. Please consult your RT administrator.\n";
    exit 1;
}

my $sc = RT::ScripCondition->new($user);

$sc->Create( Name                => 'After Hours Emergency',
             Description         => 'An emergency ticket is created after hours',
             ExecModule          => 'OnAfterHoursEmergency',
             ApplicableTransTypes => 'Create',
           );
```

Note that ApplicableTransTypes field is set to Create, ensuring that this condition is checked only when a new ticket is created. We could have done this in the condition module's IsApplicable() method, but this is more efficient.

To create a new scrip for this condition, we would pick *After Hours Emergency* from the condition drop down in the new scrip form. The action will be *Notify Other Recipients*. The actual recipients will be picked up from the template. For the template, we use the one we just created.

If we had different pager numbers for different queues, we could create several templates. Then we would set up scrips for each queue, all using the same condition and action, each with a different template.

Using TransactionBatch

Earlier, we talked about the two stages where scrips could run, TransactionCreate and TransactionBatch. The latter stage needs to be enabled in your configuration before it is available.

This might be needed, for example, if you wanted to send an email whenever any of the custom fields for a ticket were updated. Because of the way custom fields work, each change to a custom field is a separate transaction. If a ticket might have five custom fields, we do not want to send five emails every time that ticket is updated!

We can use the TransactionBatch stage to look at all of the transactions at once. Here's an example of a simple template that would run in the TransactionBatch stage:

```
{
    my @batch = @{ $Ticket->TransactionBatch };

    foreach my $txn ( @batch ) {
        if ( $txn->Type eq 'CustomField' ) {
            $OUT .= '* ' . $txn->Description . "\n";
        }
    }
    return $OUT;
}
```

This template could be used with a scrip that had this custom condition:

```
my @batch = @{ $Ticket->TransactionBatch };
foreach my $txn ( @batch ) {
    if ( $txn->Type eq 'CustomField' ) {
        return 1;
    }
}
return 0;
```

This scrip simply checks all the transactions in the batch to see if any of them changed custom fields.

The action for this scrip would be one of the Notify actions, depending on exactly who should receive the email.

This is a simple example, but it illustrates the basic idea behind the Transaction-Batch stage, which is to allow you to handle a group of transactions all at once.

A Simple Workflow

As we mentioned earlier, one of the uses for custom scrips is to implement a work-flow system in RT. Let's look at a simple example of this concept, which uses the ability to have a scrip create a new ticket.

For our example, let's assume that we have two groups of people using RT, each with their own queue. Both of these groups are working in some sort of agency that does creative work, like a graphic design firm.

The first group is the designers. Their queue has tickets like "create mockup of poster for Faye Wong's spring tour." The other group is the account representatives. They use RT to track the designer's work, so they know when things are ready for review with the clients.

It would be possible to simply transfer tickets from one queue to the other, so that when a designer wanted a representative to review their work, they would transfer the ticket to the Review queue and assign ownership to Nobody. But if we wanted to use RT for time tracking, by updating the time worked field for tickets, this could get awkward. In this case, it's better to create a new ticket for each piece of work. And of course, ideally, every time a ticket in the Design queue is closed, a new ticket in the Review queue is opened. If a given project needs additional design work, the account representative can create a new ticket in the Design queue.

To make the automatic creation of Review tickets happen, we can create a new scrip where the condition is *On Resolve*, and the action is *Create Tickets*. We just need to create a custom template that creates the correct ticket in the Review queue. That template would look something like this:

```
===Create-Ticket: design-review
Queue:      Review
Subject:    Review of { $Tickets{'TOP'}->Subject() }
Owner:      { $Tickets{'TOP'}->Requestors->UserMembersObj->Next->Id() }
Requestor:  { $Tickets{'TOP'}->OwnerObj->EmailAddress() }
RefersTo:   { $Tickets{'TOP'}->Id() }
Content:    A ticket in the Design queue has been resolved and requires review.
```

A template used by the *Create Tickets* action has a special format. It can create one or more tickets. Each ticket to be created has its own header, which in our example is the first line. The header is ===Create-Ticket: followed by a name.

If you were creating multiple tickets, then each ticket could access the tickets already created via the %Tickets hash. This is handy if you want to create several tickets and link them together. The ticket that triggered the *Create Tickets* action is always available as $Tickets{'TOP'}.

In our example, we create only one ticket. The subject of the new ticket is based on the ticket being resolved. The owner of the ticket is the first requestor of the original ticket. The requestor is the ticket's owner. We want the new ticket to have a link back to the original ticket, so we set the *RefersTo* field.

Finally, the *Content* field is the body of the new ticket. This could be combined with a custom script to send an email whenever a new ticket is created in the Review queue with an owner (as opposed to being owned by Nobody). This way the owner of the new ticket would know that it was their responsibility to review the work just completed.

Approvals

Approvals are a useful way to get tickets OK'd by management. Unlike the review tickets from the simple workflow example above, approvals are managed through a separate Approval menu. The main rules of approvals are:

- A ticket cannot be closed until all of its approvals are resolved.
- Once an approval is rejected, its original ticket is immediately rejected, and all of its other approvals are rejected as well.
- When an approval is resolved or rejected, comments from the person approving or rejecting the approval ticket are attached to the original ticket.

To set up the approval system for a queue, create a new scrip where the condition is On Create and the action is Create Tickets. The scrip should use a new template that looks like this:

```
===Create-Ticket: manager-approval
Subject:  Approval of { $Tickets{'TOP'}->Subject() }
Queue:    ___Approvals
Type:     approval
Owner:    manager@example.com
Content:  Please review and approve this request.
Depended-On-By: TOP
ENDOFCONTENT
```

From this point on, new tickets in that queue will be displayed with the status (pending approval), and the manager will receive a mail saying that there is a new ticket that needs approval. Once the manager approves it in the Approval menu, the staff can then process and resolve it as usual.

It is also possible to have multi-stage approvals, where an approval can happen only after another approval's successful resolution. For example, we can set up a CEO approval stage by editing the template above to add another paragraph of code:

```
===Create-Ticket: ceo-approval
Subject:  Approval of { $Tickets{'TOP'}->Subject() }
Queue:    ___Approvals
Type:     approval
Owner:    ceo@example.com
Content:  Please review and approve this request.
Depended-On-By: TOP
Depends-On: manager-approval
ENDOFCONTENT
```

The last line says that CEO's approval will be activated only after the successful resolution of the manager's approval. Note that you will still need the Depended-On-By: TOP line to make the original ticket depend on the CEO's approval.

The workflow for the approval system is already built into RT. RT creates the __ Approvals queue as part of its installation process, but this queue does not show up in the normal list of queues. Tickets where the Type is approval are visible only through the Approvals menu.

## CHAPTER 7

Example Configurations

In this chapter, we'll look at a number of possible applications for RT within an example company, Yoyodyne Propulsion Systems. Yoyodyne makes rocket engines and the software systems that control them. Unlike most manufacturers of rocket systems, they sell to a number of private customers. Yoyodyne has chosen RT as their enterprise-wide ticketing system for tracking everything from purchase orders to test-firings.

This walkthrough of Yoyodyne's RT configuration is fairly comprehensive, and although it could give you ideas for your own installation, nothing we recommend here should be taken as gospel. What works well at Yoyodyne might need some adjustment to be useful to your organization. It's our hope that based on Yoyodyne's working examples, you'll find new and innovative uses for RT.

Each example configuration consists of some combination of a queue, custom fields, scrips, templates, and ACLs. Chapter 5 explains how to use RT's web interface to implement these configurations.

Network and Server Operations

Yoyodyne's Operations group consists primarily of systems and network administrators (admins). They manage all of the computing and network infrastructure at Yoyodyne and were responsible for bringing RT into the organization. They use RT as an internal tool to track the work they need to do and the work they've already done.

System and network admins use the Network and Server Operations queue to track everything that goes on with Yoyodyne's technical infrastructure. An admin opens a ticket for anything that needs to be done, whether or not there's a problem involved. By updating the relevant ticket each time anyone works an issue, the team makes sure that any individual admin always can find out about the status of an issue or project, just by checking the ticket. For example, finding out what's changed on the server *bonzai.yoyodyne.com* in the past month is as simple as searching for all the tickets in the Network and Server Operations queue that mention "bonzai" in the *Hardware device affected* custom field and have been updated in the last month.

Custom Fields

Yoyodyne's staff added a number of custom fields for tickets in the Network and Server Operations queue.

Hardware device affected
> Yoyodyne's staff fill this *FreeformMultiple* field with the hostname of any piece of network hardware that this ticket references. If the ticket is about an issue on the email server *bigbooty.yoyodyne.com*, staff fill in that name. If the ticket is about the network link between the WAN routers *dimension3.yoyodyne.com* and *dimension8.yoyodyne.com*, the sysadmins fill in both of those hostnames.

Severity
> RT lets you track the priority of each ticket in the system on a general numeric scale. Yoyodyne categorizes their systems issues with a *SelectSingle* custom field on a much simpler scale: *Critical* issues prevent many people from doing their jobs. *Severe* issues prevent a few people from doing their jobs. *Important* issues may inconvenience a number of users but don't prevent anyone from doing his job. *Normal* issues inconvenience only a few users. *Minor* issues are things that easily can be deferred to later; they don't inconvenience anyone and don't have to be done anytime soon. Sometimes an issue will be upgraded to a higher severity level by a manager. For example, if the CEO's email is unavailable while all other users' mail is unaffected, it is likely that the VP of Operations will open a *Critical* ticket. In theory, this works the other way as well, but Yoyodyne's staff has never seen an issue reported with a lower Severity than it merits.

Location
> This *FreeformSingle* field lets Yoyodyne staff quickly record a physical location for a given ticket. This could be something like "machine room at the rocket test site" or "the loading dock at the main warehouse."

Vendor Ticket #
> Yoyodyne uses this *FreeformSingle* field to track what ticket number their network provider or hardware vendor has opened for a particular issue. Not every ticket will have a vendor ticket number.

Groups

Yoyodyne's staff created a single user-defined group in RT called Sysadmins. This group contains all of the systems and network administrators.

Scrips

The Network and Server Operations queue uses the scrips outlined in Table 7-1.

Table 7-1. Network and Server Operations scrips

Condition	Action	Template
On Create	Page Admins if severity is `critical`	Pager
On Correspond	Notify AdminCcs	Admin Correspondence
On Correspond	Notify Requestors	Correspondence
On Create	Autoreply to Requestors	Autoreply
On Comment	Notify AdminCcs	Admin Comment

ACLs

An ACL, or Access Control List, is a flexible and powerful way to manage access rights, based on membership in a list that has the appropriate rights assigned to it. Lists can be assigned to one another to create complex and useful access groups to suit the level of control detail required.

To allow all staff at Yoyodyne to submit tickets to RT, the administrators granted the Privileged group the following rights:

```
SeeQueue
CreateTicket
ReplyToTicket
```

Yoyodyne's Sysadmins are able to do just about everything to tickets in the Network and Server Operations queue, so the RT administrators granted the Sysadmin group the following rights:

```
ShowTicket
ShowTicketComments
ShowOutgoingEmail
Watch
WatchAsAdminCc
CreateTicket
CommentOnTicket
OwnTicket
ModifyTicket
DeleteTicket
TakeTicket
StealTicket
```

Helpdesk

Yoyodyne's corporate internal helpdesk fields a couple hundred inquiries a day by phone and by email. No matter how simple the problem report or question is, a ticket is always opened. Eighty percent of the time, the tickets are closed out immediately with a simple note like "Told the user to reboot." Having a record of every call that comes into the helpdesk has made new staffing requests much easier and has helped to identify what software and hardware are the best candidates for upgrade or replacement during the next budget year.

Custom Fields

The Helpdesk queue has several custom fields.

Hardware device affected
> Yoyodyne staff fill this *FreeformMultiple* field with the hostname of any piece of network hardware to which this ticket refers.

Severity
> Yoyodyne categorizes its helpdesk issues with the same *SelectSingle* custom field they use for systems and network administration.

Location
> This *FreeformSingle* field lets Yoyodyne staff quickly record a physical location for a given ticket. It's usually an office number.

Operating System
> This *SelectSingle* field keeps track of which operating system a given problem report is about. Generally staff only fill it out when the first technician to deal with an issue can't resolve it quickly. This makes it easy for more specialized staff to find open issues they can help resolve. When Steve, one of the Macintosh specialists, comes in in the morning, he does a quick search for all of the new or open Macintosh issues that are currently unowned and takes responsibility for them.

Scrips

RT originally was designed for use by a helpdesk, so just about all the scrips that Yoyodyne uses for the helpdesk—shown in Table 7-2—are included the RT distribution.

Table 7-2. Helpdesk scrips

Condition	Action	Template
On Create	Autoreply to Requestors	Autoreply
On Create	Notify AdminCcs	Admin Correspondence
On Correspond	Notify Requestors and Ccs	Correspondence
On Correspond	Notify AdminCcs	Admin Correspondence
On Comment	Notify AdminCcs	Admin Comment
On Create	Autoreply to Requestors	Password

Using a specialized template named *Password*, the Helpdesk queue has RT send a password for the SelfService web interface to each user the first time they submit a helpdesk ticket. If a user already has an RT account with a password, nothing will happen.

Templates

The helpdesk uses a single custom email template named Password. It's the autoreply with Password template defined in Chapter 6.

Groups

To make it easier to manage access control, all helpdesk staff is added to a Helpdesk group.

ACLs

To allow all staff at Yoyodyne to submit tickets to RT, the Privileged group has the following ACL rights:

```
SeeQueue
CreateTicket
ReplyToTicket
```

To let end users use the SelfService interface to log in, view, and update their own tickets, the Requestor role group has the following rights:

```
ShowTicket
ShowTicketHistory
```

Yoyodyne's helpdesk staff is able to do just about everything to tickets in the Helpdesk queue, so the RT administrators granted the Helpdesk group the following ACL rights:

```
ShowTicket
ShowTicketComments
ShowOutgoingEmail
Watch
WatchAsAdminCc
CreateTicket
CommentOnTicket
OwnTicket
ModifyTicket
DeleteTicket
TakeTicket
StealTicket
```

Software Engineering

Yoyodyne's software developers use RT to track defects and tasks related to their rocket control software. RT makes it easy for developers to track open issues and to dig for historical information about issues that were resolved ages ago. Any developer can open a ticket for a bug or task that needs to be handled. Development managers generally are responsible for assigning tickets to individual developers, but developers are encouraged to take responsibility for issues themselves when they have a bit of time on their hands and see something that they know how to handle.

Yoyodyne's RT administrators have hooked RT to their software version control system to let programmers update tickets as they check source code into the version control system. If you use Subversion, you can do the same thing using the RT-Integration-SVN package, which is available from your neighborhood CPAN mirror.

Custom Fields

The Software Engineering department uses custom fields more heavily than any other department within Yoyodyne. Custom fields make it easy for them to mark which product a given ticket applies to and what versions of the product are affected. When Yoyodyne's tech writers are preparing errata and release notes, the additional categorization provided by the custom fields makes it easy to find out what changed between two releases.

Platform
> This *SelectMultiple* field lets engineers flag whether a particular task or issue applies to all platforms or just Linux, Solaris, Win32, or VMS.

Severity
> This *SelectSingle* field tracks the severity of a bug. In descending order of severity, the values Yoyodyne uses are:

> *Wishlist*
>> This ticket is a feature request or a bug that's from another dimension and will never be fixed.

> *Trivial*
>> This ticket is a bug report for something relatively unimportant that's not going to get in anybody's way.

> *Normal*
>> This ticket is a bug report. It's clearly a software defect, but isn't such a big deal that it's going to delay a release or cause anyone serious trouble.

> *Serious*
>> This ticket is a bug report for something that causes the product to break but that can be worked around by an end-user without extraordinary measures.

> *Showstopper*
>> This ticket is a bug that's so severe that the product can't be released. The bug either causes data loss or the product breaks during normal, common operations.

Product

> Yoyodyne makes several different products. This *SelectSingle* field lets engineers tag whether a ticket refers to their Rocket Guidance Software, Mission Control Console, or Advanced Targeting Platform.

Broken In

> This *FreeformMultiple* field lets developers manually key in the version numbers of releases that a bug is known to exist in, one per line. For tickets that aren't bugs, this field is left empty. Future releases of RT may enable this field to become a cascading field, one that is automatically populated with the correct list of version numbers corresponding to the value in the Product field.

Target Release

> Every bug or task is assigned a Target Release. This *FreeformSingle* field tracks the version number of the release this ticket is expected to handle.

Groups

The Software Engineering team has a single group, Software Engineering, to define both the access control for their queue and the list of people who should get mail when someone updates a ticket. Everyone on the team is a member of this group. Yoyodyne's RT administrators added this group as an AdminCc for the Software Engineering queue, so that everyone can get mail about every ticket update using only standard scrips.

Scrips

Yoyodyne's developers are all email junkies. Most of their interaction with RT is via the email gateway. When a manager assigns a bug to a given developer, the developer usually does a bit of exploratory work to figure out what it will take to fix the bug and updates the ticket by email. Then RT automatically will distribute that mail to the entire development team for comment. When a developer checks in new code, the version control system integration sends out a ticket update to the entire development team with details of the check-in. The scrips for the Software Engineering queue shown in Table 7-3 are designed to make this process as simple and transparent as possible.

Table 7-3. Software Engineering scrips

Condition	Action	Template
On Create	Autoreply to Requestors	Autoreply
On Create	Notify AdminCcs	Admin Correspondence
On Correspond	Notify AdminCcs	Admin Correspondence
On Comment	Notify AdminCcs	Admin Comment
On Owner Change	Notify Owner	Transaction

The first scrip ensures that when someone enters a new bug or task into the Software Engineering queue, they get an acknowledgement by email. The second and third scrips make sure that all the mail about a particular issue gets sent to all of the queue's AdminCcs. Yoyodyne's engineers don't use comments much inside RT, but the fourth scrip makes sure that everyone gets notified when someone accidentally enters one. The last scrip makes sure that the developer knows that he's been assigned a bug or task.

ACLs

All software engineers have the same rights within the Software Engineering queue. Yoyodyne's RT administrators have granted the Software Engineering group the following rights for this queue:

```
ShowTicket
ShowTicketComments
ShowOutgoingEmail
Watch
WatchAsAdminCc
CreateTicket
CommentOnTicket
OwnTicket
ModifyTicket
DeleteTicket
TakeTicket
StealTicket
```

Customer Service

Every so often, a customer has a question about how to use their rocket or whether their rocket is rated for a specific mission. Yoyodyne takes good customer service very seriously and does everything it can to make sure that every customer gets her questions answered quickly and correctly. An important part of that strategy is tracking every incoming support request with RT. Emailed support requests flow directly into RT through the email gateway. Customer Service staff open tickets for issues that come in by email.

By reviewing all the requests that come through the Customer Service team, Yoyodyne's engineers are better able to plan how to make their rockets more robust and easier to use. The sales team leads occasionally go through the past few months' tickets in the Customer Service queue to decide which customers might need some buttering up after they've had a test or a launch go awry.

Custom Fields

Yoyodyne's Customer Service team uses a pair of custom fields to keep track of which products users are reporting issues with. Both fields are used heavily during

---

the reporting process and when evaluating possible hardware or software defects, but they aren't used much in the immediate triage process. The two fields are:

Model
> This *SelectSingle* field lets staff track which sort of hardware the user is having trouble with.

Serial Number
> Yoyodyne staff use this *FreeformSingle* field to track which specific bit of hardware or software a ticket is about.

Groups

The Customer Service queue is managed primarily by Customer Service staff. There are a couple of engineers who are responsible for handling escalated issues, and the Customer Service staff will sometimes assign issues to those engineers. Additionally, certain Engineering and Sales managers are allowed to peek into the queue.

To simplify queue administration, Yoyodyne set up RT groups for each of these roles:

Customer Service Reps
> Every Customer Service Representative is a member of this group.

Customer Service Engineers
> These engineers have regular duties outside the customer service team, but from time to time will be called upon to deal with complex user issues.

Customer Service Reviewers
> This group consists of the engineering and sales managers who are allowed to look at support requests but not modify them.

ACLs

The Everyone group is granted certain rights to the Customer Service queue to allow end-users to report and correspond on issues:

```
CreateTicket
ReplyToTicket
```

The Customer Service Reps group is granted full power to manage tickets in this queue, so this group needs to be assigned a full range of ACL rights:

```
CommentOnTicket
CreateTicket
DeleteTicket
ModifyTicket
OwnTicket
ReplyToTicket
SeeQueue
ShowOutgoingEmail
```

```
ShowTicket
ShowTicketComments
ShowTicketHistory
StealTicket
TakeTicket
Watch
WatchAsAdminCc
```

Customer Service Engineers have the exact same ACL rights as Customer Service Reps:

```
CommentOnTicket
CreateTicket
DeleteTicket
ModifyTicket
OwnTicket
ReplyToTicket
SeeQueue
ShowOutgoingEmail
ShowTicket
ShowTicketComments
ShowTicketHistory
StealTicket
TakeTicket
Watch
WatchAsAdminCc
```

Customer Service Reviewers are allowed to look at everything in the Customer Service queue, but aren't allowed to change anything, so the ACL rights assigned to them are a bit more limited:

```
SeeQueue
ShowOutgoingEmail
ShowTicket
ShowTicketComments
ShowTicketHistory
Watch
WatchAsAdminCc
```

Scrips

Customer Service reps work pretty much entirely within the RT user interface, so RT has been configured not to firehose the entire team with mail about every issue. Instead, only the owner of a ticket is notified. Additionally, whenever a ticket is given to someone to handle, he gets a notification. This makes sure that the Customer Service Engineers know about issues they need to handle. Table 7-4 shows the scrips that apply to the Customer Service queue.

Table 7-4. Customer Service scrips

Condition	Action	Template
On Create	Autoreply to Requestors	Autoreply
On Correspond	Notify Requestors and Ccs	Correspondence

Table 7-4. Customer Service scrips (continued)

Condition	Action	Template
On Correspond	Notify Owner	Admin Correspondence
On Comment	Notify Owner	Admin Comment
On Owner Change	Notify Owner	Transaction

Emergency Support

Like every product ever built by any company, sometimes customers have critical issues with Yoyodyne rockets they need solved *right now*, no matter what time of day or night it is. Yoyodyne uses RT to make sure that the right people get paged when a customer reports an issue by email or phone. (Yoyodyne's RT administrators set up their voicemail system to email RT a copy of any message left in an emergency voicemail box.)

Using an Emergency Support queue gives the staff handling an urgent customer issue a central repository to store important data while they dig into and resolve the problem. Once the customer's rocket is back on course, Yoyodyne's managment staff has an accurate record of how long it took their staff to respond and how quickly they managed to help the customer resolve the issue.

Templates

Yoyodyne's RT administrators created the following custom Emergency Pager template to send email to the emergency-response staff. It also pages whichever team member is unlucky enough to have the on-call pager when the new ticket comes in.

```
To: support-emergency-pager@yoyodynepropulsion.com
Subject: 911 - Ticket { $Ticket->Id( ) }

A new emergency ticket has been opened. Time to get to work!
```

Groups

To make sure that all customer service reps and engineers who deal with customer service get notified on just about any update to a ticket about a support emergency, Yoyodyne made the Customer Service Reps and Customer Service Engineers Admin-Ccs for the Emergency Support Queue.

Scrips

Emergency Support is configured the same as the regular support queue. It adds one scrip, the first row in Table 7-5, to page the on-call support engineer.

Table 7-5. Emergency Support scrips

Condition	Action	Template
On Create	Notify AdminCcs	Emergency Pager
On Create	Autoreply to Requestors	Autoreply
On Correspond	Notify Requestors and Ccs	Correspondence
On Correspond	Notify AdminCcs	Admin Correspondence
On Comment	Notify AdminCcs	Admin Comment
On Owner Change	Notify Owner	Transaction

ACLs

The Everyone group is granted certain rights to the emergency support queue to make sure that a customer reporting an emergency issue never gets a "Permission Denied" error. This means that occasionally a bit of spam or a non-customer sends email to the emergency support queue, but it's worth it to make sure that Yoyodyne never misses a customer emergency. The Everyone group has the following rights:

```
CreateTicket
ReplyToTicket
```

The Customer Service Reps and Customer Service Engineers groups are granted full power to manage tickets in the Emergency Support queue with the following rights:

```
CommentOnTicket
CreateTicket
DeleteTicket
ModifyTicket
OwnTicket
ReplyToTicket
SeeQueue
ShowOutgoingEmail
ShowTicket
ShowTicketComments
ShowTicketHistory
StealTicket
TakeTicket
Watch
WatchAsAdminCc
```

Sales Inquiries

Yoyodyne makes some of the most popular rockets in the world. They get inquiries from governments and corporations around the world. They also get a lot of email from crackpots. The sales team uses RT to make sure that no legitimate sales inquiry gets lost.

Custom Fields

The sales team started out tagging each inquiry with a custom field for metrics purposes, but it quickly discovered that the vast majority of initial inbound sales inquiries were simple requests for literature and the cute rocket toys that they give away at tradeshows. Rather than spend energy categorizing these requests, Yoyodyne has an intern who mines the inbound inquiries for new sales leads each week and moves likely candidates to a Sales Leads queue for senior salespeople to view.

Groups

Yoyodyne's RT administrators created a single group called Salesforce and made every salesperson and sales intern a member of that group.

ACLs

To make sure that any potential customer can inquire about buying rockets, The Everyone group is granted the following rights:

```
SeeQueue
CreateTicket
ReplyToTicket
```

The Salesforce group has the following rights:

```
TakeTicket
ShowTicket
ShowTicketComments
OwnTicket
ModifyTicket
Watch
WatchAsAdminCc
ShowOutgoingEmail
StealTicket
ReplyToTicket
```

Templates

To make sure that Yoyodyne presents the right impression to possible customers, the sales team crafted a custom Sales Autoreply template that answers some of the most frequent questions about buying rockets from Yoyodyne.

Scrips

The Sales Inquiries queue gets a lot of mail. A basic set of scrips makes sure that potential customers get mail sent by Yoyodyne. Yoyodyne interns who own a given inquiry also get mail any time a potential customer writes back. Due to the volume of initial inquiries, there's no scrip to notify Yoyodyne staff on ticket creation; interns pick up new tickets from the web interface. The scrips in the Sales Inquiries are listed in Table 7-6.

Table 7-6. Sales Inquiries scrips

Condition	Action	Template
On Create	Autoreply to Requestors	Sales Autoreply
On Correspond	Notify Requestors and Ccs	Correspondence
On Correspond	Notify Owner	Admin Correspondence
On Comment	Notify Owner	Admin Comment

Human Resources

As the premiere creator of rocket engines in the world, Yoyodyne's HR department is under a constant barrage of resumes from job applicants. Each resume comes to *resumes@yoyodynepropulsion.com* and gets a prompt autoreply thanking the applicant for their interest in the rocket propulsion industry. Behind the scenes, an intern in the HR department does a first pass through incoming resumes, looking for resumes that either match currently open job postings or that are clearly not up to Yoyodyne's high standards. Resumes matching an existing posting are given to the hiring manager for that posting for review. If a resume doesn't merit further consideration, its status is set to rejected.

Due to the sheer number of resumes that are submitted to Yoyodyne each week, the Resumes queue doesn't ever email Yoyodyne staff.

Groups

The HR department maintains two groups for their Resumes queue. The HR Team group includes all members of the HR team. The Hiring Managers group includes all of the hiring managers.

ACLs

In order for potential new hires to submit their resumes to Yoyodyne, it's important to grant the Everyone group the following ACL rights:

```
CreateTicket
ReplyToTicket
```

The HR Team is allowed to work their magic on any resume that comes in, so they all need to have at least the following ACL rights:

```
CommentOnTicket
CreateTicket
DeleteTicket
ModifyTicket
```

```
OwnTicket
ReplyToTicket
SeeQueue
ShowOutgoingEmail
ShowTicket
ShowTicketComments
ShowTicketHistory
StealTicket
TakeTicket
Watch
WatchAsAdminCc
```

Hiring managers are allowed to own individual resumes, but they aren't allowed to look through incoming resumes on their own, so they need to have a minimal set of ACLs:

```
OwnTicket
SeeQueue
```

Once individual hiring managers have been made the owner of an individual resume, they're allowed to comment on the resume and otherwise update the ticket, so their ACLs are extended to include:

```
CommentOnTicket
ModifyTicket
ReplyToTicket
ShowOutgoingEmail
ShowTicket
ShowTicketComments
ShowTicketHistory
Watch
WatchAsAdminCc
```

Templates

Yoyodyne's HR department created a simple Resume Autoreply template which essentially reads:

```
Thanks for sending us your resume.

We've received it and are trying to find you a great job here. Don't
call us. We'll call you.
```

Scrips

Because the Resumes queue is designed not to send much mail, only the single scrip in Table 7-7 is needed.

Table 7-7. Resumes scrip

Condition	Action	Template
On Create	AutoReply to Requestors	Resume Autoreply

This scrip uses the template that the HR department created above to reassure job applicants that their resume didn't get lost in the mail.

Finance

In the old days, Yoyodyne's Accounts Receivable (AR) department kept a paper file of all outstanding invoices. This worked well enough when customers needed paper invoices. In the past few years, it's become somewhat cumbersome to use paper files for invoices, since most customers have been accepting electronic invoices by email. Yoyodyne's AR department now uses an RT queue to track both electronic and paper invoices.

Each time a new rocket is sold to a customer, a clerk opens a new ticket in the Accounts Receivable queue with the customer's Accounts Payable department as the requestor. He creates a new invoice with the ticket ID as the invoice number and attaches the newly generated invoice to a ticket update. RT automatically sends the invoice to the customer and tracks any future correspondence by email. When a customer's check or wire transfer clears, an AR clerk updates the ticket with the payment information, sends a thank-you note to the customer, and resolves the ticket.

Each morning, a clerk scans the currently open tickets in the AR queue to make sure there's nothing overdue or outstanding that needs attention.

Custom Fields

Yoyodyne's staff added several custom fields for tickets in the Accounts Receivable queue.

Customer Purchase order #
> This *FreeformSingle* field tracks the customer PO number associated with this invoice.

Total cost
> When creating a ticket, a clerk fills in this *FreeformSingle* field with the total dollar figure on the invoice, to make it easy to see which outstanding invoices might need the most attention.

Payment terms
> Yoyodyne supplies to both the government and to private corporations. Some organizations have negotiated different payment terms. This *SelectSingle* field lets an AR clerk note whether an invoice is due in 30, 60, or 90 days.

Payment date
> When a customer finally pays up, a clerk fills in this *FreeformSingle* field with the date the payment was made by the customer.

Payment ID
> Yoyodyne keeps track of the check or wire transfer number associated with each invoice payment in this *FreeformSingle* field.

Scrips

The Accounts Receivable queue is designed to make sure that it's easy for Yoyodyne to communicate with (possibly delinquent) customers about their outstanding invoices. Its scrips are fairly generic, with the exception of the On Create scrip which has been tweaked to send outgoing mail on ticket creation rather than simply replying to an incoming message. The scrips are listed in Table 7-8.

Table 7-8. Accounts Receivable scrips

Condition	Action	Template
On Create	Notify Requestors and Ccs	Correspondence
On Create	Notify AdminCcs	Admin Correspondence
On Correspond	Notify Requestors and Ccs	Correspondence
On Correspond	Notify AdminCcs	Admin Correspondence
On Comment	Notify AdminCcs	Admin Comment

Groups

Yoyodyne created a group for the AR department called (somewhat unsurprisingly) Accounts Receivable. Everyone on the AR team should be able to manage tickets and get copied on all invoice-related correspondence, so the Accounts Receivable group has been made an AdminCc of the Accounts Receivable queue.

ACLs

To allow customers to reply to invoices sent out by mail, Yoyodyne has granted the Everyone group the following ACL right:

```
ReplyToTicket
```

To allow the AR team to manage invoices fully, the RT administrators granted the Accounts Receivable group the following ACL rights:

```
CommentOnTicket
CreateTicket
DeleteTicket
ModifyTicket
OwnTicket
ReplyToTicket
SeeQueue
ShowOutgoingEmail
ShowTicket
ShowTicketComments
StealTicket
TakeTicket
Watch
WatchAsAdminCc
```

The Paperless Office

Like most growing rocket propulsion companies, Yoyodyne is a busy place. People are rushing constantly between the main office downtown and the engineering office at the testing range to check up on the latest rocket tests, which means that nobody is ever at their desk to take a phone call. Yoyodyne used to use those little pink "While you were out" forms but people kept missing phone calls, because the little pink notes never quite managed to catch up with their intended recipients.

Yoyodyne's RT administrators set up a new queue called Messages that lets any Yoyodyne staffer take a message for any other. No matter where they are, Yoyodyne staff can now get a quick rundown of all the phone calls they haven't returned.

Custom Fields

Yoyodyne uses a set of custom fields to mimic the boxes on their "While you were out" forms. They're just there to give someone recording a phone call a place to record the important information. You may want to track more or different things. Yoyodyne's fields are:

Caller name
> A *FreeformSingle* field to record the caller's name.

Caller organization
> A *FreeformSingle* field to record the caller's organization.

Caller phone number
> A *FreeformSingle* field to record the caller's phone number.

Best time to call back
> A *FreeformSingle* field in case the caller left some information about when to contact them.

Contact method
> This *SelectMultiple* custom field lets the person taking the message record simple notes about the call with just a few clicks. Yoyodyne's list of options includes: *Called*, *Returned your call*, *Will call back*, and *Came by*.

Templates

Folks at Yoyodyne who answer the phone need an email template to mimic the little pink paper forms that they're replacing. The template needs to display the various custom fields the administrators have set up. Yoyodyne went with a Messages template that looks like this:

```
Messages:

{
    $CustomFields = $Ticket->QueueObj->CustomFields();
    while (my $CustomField = $CustomFields->Next()) {
```

```
        my $Values = $Ticket->CustomFieldValues($CustomField->Id());
        $OUT .= $CustomField->Name . ": ";
        while (my $Value = $Values->Next()) {
            $OUT .= $Value->Content . " "
        }
    }
}

For full details, go to:

{ $RT::WebURL }Ticket/Display.html?id={ $Ticket->Id() }
```

Scrips

You only get one of those little pink notes for each missed call. Likewise, the Messages queue is set up with a single scrip, shown in Table 7-9.

Table 7-9. Messages scrip

Condition	Action	Template
On Create	Notify Owner	Messages

ACLs

Messages should be easy for anyone to enter, but they should be private, so that only their intended recipients can see the messages and resolve them. To satisfy these two goals, Yoyodyne grants both the Privileged Users and Owner built-in groups rights to the Messages queue. The Privileged Users group has the following rights:

```
SeeQueue
CreateTicket
OwnTicket
```

The Owner group has the following rights:

```
ShowTicket
ShowTicketHistory
ShowTicketComments
ModifyTicket
```

Personal To-Do Lists

Everybody at Yoyodyne used to line their desks in scrawled sticky notes, covering everything from "Bring NASA memo to dev meeting" to "Get milk on the way home." The cleaners would find little yellow pieces of paper on the floor with something that looked like writing on them and stick them to the closest desk—which was rarely the right desk.

As part of its continuing program to save the environment and help staff keep track of things that need to be done, Yoyodyne decided to replace a couple thousand two-inch pads of paper with RT. The Todo queue in Yoyodyne's RT instance is designed to let staff track their own notes, but it is specifically set up so that nobody can see anyone else's notes. Yoyodyne has policies prohibiting personal use of corporate resources, but the legal department has blessed this use of RT as equivalent to writing out grocery lists on corporate note pads. If you decide to follow Yoyodyne's example here, make sure that you're not encouraging your users to violate corporate policies.

The Todo queue is set up to be as similar to paper notes as possible. There are no custom fields. No email gets sent out about Todo items. Nobody but the owner of each note can see its content.

ACLs

To let everyone at Yoyodyne use the Todo queue, the administrators granted Privileged Users the following ACL rights:

```
SeeQueue
CreateTicket
OwnTicket
```

To ensure that only the owner of a Todo item can check it off (or even see that it exists), the administrators have given Owner the following ACL rights:

```
CommentOnTicket
ShowTicket
ShowTicketComments
ReplyToTicket
ModifyTicket
```

Conclusion

Hopefully, this whirlwind tour of Yoyodyne's RT configuration has helped make some of RT's concepts a little more clear and possibly given you some ideas on how you'd like to structure your own RT instance.

## CHAPTER 8

Architecture

RT is built like a layer cake. Each layer has no innate knowledge of what sits on top of it.* This chapter takes a tour of RT's structure and then a more detailed look at RT's database and object models.

Quick Overview

Before we get into the nitty gritty details of how RT is put together, let's take a quick look at the RT layer cake and see what we get out of each layer. Figure 8-1 shows the layers and how they fit together.

SQL Database

> Behind everything that RT does, there's an SQL database. This database stores all of RT's data and metadata. Some SQL databases provide their own procedural languages that allow developers to implement large applications entirely inside the database. This has the disadvantage of tying an application tightly to a specific database engine, such as MySQL or Oracle. RT takes a different tack, using the database as a datastore. Because of this, RT is able to run on top of a number of different database engines, each of which has different strengths. RT works to make sure that data stored in SQL is relatively easy to query using other tools, though we strongly recommend that you not alter the database by hand.

DBI

> Perl's DBI is the standard SQL Database Interface for Perl programs. It defines an interface that various and sundry database drivers (DBDs) implement in a largely consistent manner. In addition to MySQL, Postgres, and Oracle, you'll find DBD modules that let you talk to LDAP, flat text files, and even Google as if

---

* There are a couple of places where this isn't quite true yet, but it's being improved with each new version.

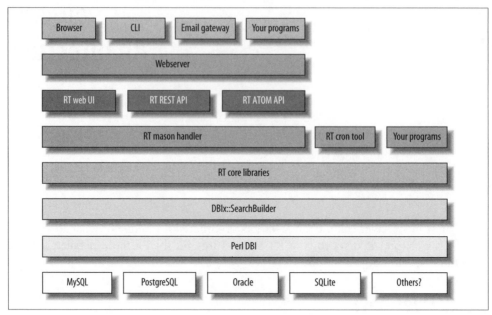

Figure 8-1. The RT layer cake

they were SQL databases. If you come from the Java world, you can think of DBI as Perl's equivalent to JDBC.

DBIx::SearchBuilder

> DBIx::SearchBuilder is the secret sauce that lets an object-oriented application like RT talk to a table-oriented relational database. SearchBuilder presents a simple object-oriented API to Perl programs and translates those API calls into SQL statements tuned for the specific database. A row from any given database table can be accessed via a subclass of DBIx::SearchBuilder::Record. To search for and work with sets of records all at once, RT provides a Collection class for each database table, which is a subclass of DBIx::SearchBuilder itself.

RT application platform libraries

> Until now, we've only talked about RT as a ticketing system. Once you start looking at the architecture and APIs, you'll quickly discover that there's a whole application platform under the hood in addition to the ticketing system.

> RT's application platform libraries are the guts of RT. They provide database connectivity, logging infrastructure, users, groups, access control, links, and a few other bits. While the ticketing system uses the RT application platform, it's not the only application that does so. RTFM* is a knowledge-base tool that uses the RT application platform to implement an entirely different application.

---

* The RT FAQ Manager. It doesn't mean anything else, really!

RT ticketing system libraries

    RT's ticketing system libraries use the RT application platform as a base to provide tickets, transactions, attachments, custom fields, and queues. The ticketing system defines groups and access control rights and a type of link that teaches the application platform how to deal with links between ticket objects.

Mason handler

    The Mason handler is one of many possible applications that runs on top of the RT Core libraries. It provides a wrapper around the Mason templating system.* Mason is conceptually similar to ASP, PHP, or JSP, but for Perl.

    RT comes with two main sets of Mason templates out of the box: user interface templates, which are designed for end users to interact with their browsers, and REST templates, which are designed to be easy for other software to interact with. As of version 3.4, the REST templates are designed to present information in RFC822 format, which anything can parse.

    Right now, the Mason templates for the RT application platform and RT ticketing system are very tightly integrated, but moving forward, the templates are changing to improve how they are broken out.

HTTP Clients

    RT has three HTTP clients: a web browser, the email gateway, and the command-line interface. Most users interact with RT using their browsers. RT's email gateway is a tiny Perl script that your mail server runs every time an email message destined for RT comes in. The email gateway, in turn, dispatches the message to your RT server over HTTP or HTTPS. It waits around for the RT server to confirm receipt of the message and then exits.

    RT's command-line interface is a web browser. But not like you're imagining. The CLI communicates with RT over the web, using the same authentication system as the rest of RT, so you can use it from anywhere that you can use RT's web interface. Like any other web client, it uses GET and POST to download from and upload to your RT server.

Filesystem Layout

In the next sections and chapters, we'll dive into RT's internals to get a better sense of how RT is put together. As you're reading, it may be useful to refer to RT's source code. All the paths we talk about will be relative to your RT installation path. By default, RT is installed into */opt/rt3*, but you or your system administrator may have installed it elsewhere. Some flavors of Unix—such as Debian Linux and FreeBSD—

---

* Dave Rolsky and Ken Williams's *Embedding Perl in HTML with Mason (O'Reilly)* is the canonical source for everything about Mason.

package RT and install its code and configuration files into locations that fit system policy.

lib/

Standard Perl libraries live in *lib/*. *RT.pm* contains RT's basic initialization routines. It reads RT's configuration file, sets up connections to the database and logging system, and loads system-internal objects.

RT's other Perl libraries live inside the *RT/* subdirectory of *lib*. To add RT-specific behavior, both *RT/Record.pm* and *RT/SearchBuilder.pm* subclass `DBIx::SearchBuilder` and `DBIx::SearchBuilder::Record::Cachable`, respectively. *RT/Interface/Web.pm* handles many of the details of initialization of RT's Mason handler and provides a number of helper functions for the Mason Interface. *RT/Interface/REST.pm* provides helper functions for RT's REST-based web services framework. *RT/Interface/Email.pm* provides routines for handling incoming email messages and converting them into RT's preferred formats and encodings.

Standard lexicon files live in *lib/RT/I18N/*. Lexicon files contain translations of RT into languages other than English. They're in the extended GNU Gettext format that `Locale::Maketext::Lexicon` supports.

share/html/

Standard Mason components live in *share/html/*.

bin/

Executable RT programs live in *bin/*. `rt` is the RT command-line tool. It talks to your RT server via HTTP or HTTPS. You can copy it to other servers or your desktop to run. `rt-crontool` lets you script actions like escalations or reminder email using your system's *cron* facility. You can use `rt-mailgate` to funnel incoming email into RT. Like `rt`, it can run on any server (such as your mail server) that has Perl installed. `webmux.pl` is the mod_perl handler for RT. `mason_handler.fcgi` is the FastCGI handler for RT. `standalone_httpd` is a full RT webserver in a single tiny Perl script. It's useful for testing out RT or for your development environment. Because it's a non-forking, non-threaded Perl script, it might not stand up to full-scale production use.

sbin/

RT system programs live in *sbin/*. These tools are used during initial installation of RT. They should almost never be needed during regular use of RT. `rt-test-dependencies` is a tool to help verify that you've installed all the Perl modules RT needs to run and to help you install any that you happen to be missing. `rt-setup-database` is the RT helper script that sets up a database schema, ACLs, and data for RT or any RT extensions that touch the database.

var/

Mason cache data lives in *var/mason_data/*. Under some database backends, session data and locks may be stored under *var/session_data/*. If you are using the SQLite backend, its database is under *var/* by default, such as the file *var/rt3*.

---

etc/

Configuration files live in *etc/*. *RT_Config.pm* lists out all of RT's default configuration parameters. Database configuration parameters are set automatically by RT's *configure* script, but just about everything else is the factory default.

When RT starts up, it looks in *RT_Config.pm* and then overrides the defaults it finds there with local configuration from *RT_SiteConfig.pm*. This way, you can add any RT configuration you want to *RT_SiteConfig.pm*, rather than hand-editing the *RT_Config.pm* file and merging changes every time you upgrade.

The initial database schema also lives in *etc/*, in multiple different *schema.** files customized for each database platform.

local/

Site-local Perl libraries live in *local/lib/*. Site-local Mason components live in *local/html/*. Site-local lexicon files live in *local/po/*.

Unicode

Before RT 3.0, RT was language-agnostic. The user interface was in English,[*] and RT didn't do anything special with the text entered by users. As long as you only used the web interface, it worked OK. Users in Japan could enter text in Japanese. Users in Spain could enter text in Spanish. When RT tried to send mail, the recipient wouldn't be able to read it, since RT didn't know enough about the content of the message to correctly label it.

RT 3.0 changed all that. The interface has been fully internationalized,[†] and we've standardized on Unicode and the 8-bit UTF-8 encoding. This means that you can use English, Spanish, Russian, Japanese, Korean, and Chinese in the same message, and RT will store and display them just fine.

When a user connects to RT's web interface, RT tells his browser that it should speak to RT in UTF-8. Because the web came into being after the advent of Unicode, most every web browser knows how to speak UTF-8.

Sadly, the situation isn't so rosy in the world of email. Every language has its own encoding, sometimes even two or three of them. For email, RT has to do all of the hard work. When it receives an email message, it has a look at the message headers to see if the sender told us what encoding they were using. If the sender didn't tell RT, it uses the Perl module Encode::Guess to look at the message's content and guess what the most likely encoding is. Once RT knows what encoding an incoming message is in, it converts the message to UTF-8. When sending messages back out, RT looks at a site's list of preferred encodings, picks the most apropriate one, and re-encodes the message.

---

[*] End users painstakingly translated the entire application into three or four different languages.

[†] Well, almost fully, it doesn't deal quite right with right-to-left languages like Hebrew and Arabic yet.

Logical and Object Model

This section takes a tour of RT's logical model, shown in Figure 8-2. RT maps its logical model closely to its object model, so we've condensed the details of the object and logical models throughout the section.

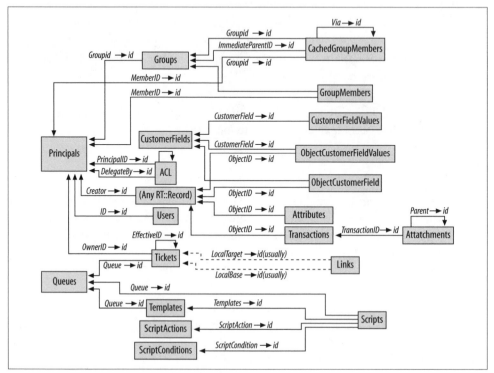

Figure 8-2. The RT Logical Model

Every RT object has a field called ID. This field is an integer that's automatically set to a unique value when an object is created and never changes. RT uses these values internally as keys to objects. Additionally, many of RT's objects have fields called Creator, Created, LastUpdated, and LastUpdatedBy. These fields automatically track the users who created and most recently updated these objects and the times of those actions. For clarity, we've skipped over those fields in the schema listings below.

Each of the database tables we discuss here corresponds to two RT objects, a record class and a collection class. The methods for each of these classes are split up into several files; see "Overlays" in Chapter 10 for more details. Method-level documentation for each class is available in Perl's *perldoc* format. Each collection class is named the same as RT's database table for that sort of object. Each record class is named for the singular version of the collection. So if you're interested in users, for example, you want to look at both `RT::Users` and `RT::User`. By default, the primary file for each of these classes lives in */opt/rt3/lib/RT/*.

The documentation in both the record and the collection modules gives an overview of the database schema for the class and provides pointers to other files that contain class methods and documentation:

```
perldoc /opt/rt3/lib/RT/User.pm
```

and

```
perldoc /opt/rt3/lib/RT/Users.pm
```

Each of these files will give you an overview of the database schema for the class, as well as provide pointers to other files that contain class methods and documentation.

Users

In RT, a user is any individual who can perform actions within the system. Any time you create, modify, look at, or delete an object, you need to do it as a user.

Out of the box, RT comes with three special users:

RT_System
> RT uses the RT_System user to perform actions as the system itself. This includes looking up data for internal use—when you really don't want access control checks to deny the system access to its own data—as well as automatically reopening a closed ticket when a user sends in email about that ticket. Inside RT, you always can access RT_System as `$RT::SystemUser`.

Nobody
> RT uses the Nobody user primarily to mark tickets that have no owner. For consistency, it's important that tickets always be owned by somebody, even if that somebody is a dummy user. Inside RT, you can access Nobody as `$RT::Nobody`.

root
> Out of the box, RT comes standard with a single user account called *root* whose password is *password*. On Unix systems, root is the superuser. Long, long ago, RT used unix system accounts instead of its own account system. The Unix-y name of this account is a holdover from those days. Once you've got an RT system up and running, nothing internal depends on the name root. There isn't a global object in RT for the root user.

Users have the following fields:

Name
> Every user in RT has a Name, which is guaranteed to be unique. While RT doesn't reference users directly by Name, users authenticate to RT and search for other users by Name.

EmailAddress

A user's EmailAddress is used by RT to attach incoming email messages to a user account upon receipt. It's also used by RT to figure out where to send outgoing mail when tickets are updated. No two users may have the same email address, although it's fine to have many users with no email address.

Password

While RT supports external access control mechanisms, many sites don't have a universal authentication framework, so RT provides its own password-based system. Internally, RT stores an MD5 hash of a user's password in the Password field but never exposes it directly to end-users. Unlike most other fields, Password is write-only. RT provides SetPassword and IsPassword methods but not a Password method. RT treats passwords such as *NO-PASSWORD and *LOCK* as locked passwords and never allows password-based access to accounts with such passwords.

Comments

RT is often used in a customer-service scenario, where it's important to be able to keep notes about users. The Comments field is a scratch-pad about a user, but it isn't visible to that user unless they're part of the Privileged group.

Signature

When composing mail from within the web interface, RT automatically will append a user's Signature to the message.

RealName

In a number of situations, RT will display a user's RealName, rather than their Name or EmailAddress.

Lang

RT's web interface provides browser-based language negotiation features, but it's sometimes useful to override that with a user's preferred language. The Lang field stores an RFC3066-style language tag.

Gecos

RT provides functionality to allow command-line tools written around the RT framework to map the current Unix username to an RT user's Gecos field.

NickName, Organization, HomePhone, WorkPhone, MobilePhone, PagerPhone, Address1, Address2, City, State, Zip, Country, FreeformContactInfo

RT provides these fields to allow sites to use it as a contact management system. They're not used internally.

EmailEncoding, WebEncoding, ExternalContactInfoId, ContactInfoSystem, ExternalAuthId, AuthSystem, Timezone, PGPKey

RT doesn't currently use these fields.

Groups

A collection of users and other groups can be assigned rights, made watchers of tickets, and so on. Groups can contain users and groups. Groups can't contain themselves.

Groups have the following fields:

Name

> Every group in RT has a name, purely for human convenience. Internally, RT doesn't care about group names.

Description

> Likewise, the Description is provided so that users know what a particular group is for.

Domain

> Many parts of RT use the groups system for a wide variety of different purposes. Domain is a high level way to mark what type each group is.

ACLEquivalence

> Internally, RT's access control system only grants rights to groups. When first created, every user has an ACL equivalence group created with only that user as a member. Whenever RT's API is used to grant rights to an individual user, the right is really granted to that user's ACL equivalence group.

SystemInternal

> RT keeps track of certain user attributes with system-wide meta-groups. Upon installation, RT creates three of these SystemInternal metagroups: Everyone, Privileged, and Unprivileged. Every single user is added as a member of the Everyone group and either the Privileged or Unprivileged group. If a user is Unprivileged, they can't be granted rights directly, and RT's web frontend automatically shunts them to a restricted self-service frontend upon login.

UserDefined

> UserDefined groups are system-wide groups created by local staff. Generally, they're used as a system managment convenience. Rights are granted to groups, rather than individual users, and groups are made Ccs or AdminCcs of Tickets or Queues. This makes it easier for administrators to track who can perform actions or who will receive email on a specific topic.

Personal

> Personal groups are defined by individual users for their own personal use. Currently, they're used only by the Delegation system to allow users to delegate rights to other users or groups.

`RT::System-Role`, `RT::Queue-Role` *and* `RT::Ticket-Role`

> Role groups are designed to allow administrators to grant rights to a role and configure mailing rules for a role at either the System or Queue level and have that configuration apply to every user who is operating in that role for

a given ticket or queue. As of RT 3.0, the possible roles are Requestor, Cc, AdminCc, and Owner.

Type

For `ACLEquivalence` groups, the group's type is `'UserEquiv'`.

For `SystemInternal` groups, the group's type is one of `'Everyone'`, `'Privileged'`, or `'Unprivileged'`.

For each of the role groups, the type is one of `Owner`, `Requestor`, `Cc`, or `AdminCc`.

For `Personal` groups, the type is always `""` (an empty string).

Instance

For `ACLEquivalence` and `Personal` groups, the group's instance is the user's ID.

For `SystemInternal` and `UserDefined` groups, the group's instance is always 0.

For `RT::Ticket-Role` groups, the group's instance is the Ticket's ID.

For `RT::Queue-Role` groups, the group's instance is the Queue's ID.

For `RT::System-Role` groups, the group's instance is always 1.

Principals

In RT, each user or group is a type of Principal. Principals are an abstraction that RT uses internally so that rights can be granted to both users and groups and so that both users and groups can be members of a group.

Principals have the following fields:

PrincipalType

A principal's type is always one of User or Group. It tells RT which sort of object this Principal is. Because a Principal's ID is always the same as the ID of the associated user or group object, it would be possible (but slow) to deduce this information on the fly.

Disabled

Sometimes a user or group is no longer needed. If you simply deleted it from the database, you'd lose information about what that user or group did in the past. RT provides the Disabled field, which lets you specify that a Principal and its associated user or group is no longer in play.

ObjectId

A principal's ObjectId is always the same as its ID. At one point, a User's ID wasn't the same as the ID of the Principal object. You should never be looking at or using a Principal's ObjectId.

GroupMembers

The GroupMembers table keeps track of all the users and groups that are members of a group. Generally, developers will interact with the GroupMembers table through the API provided by group objects.

GroupId
> GroupId refers to the group where the member belongs. It points to the ID of a group object.

MemberId
> MemberId is the ID of a Principal that is a member of the group referenced by the GroupId.

CachedGroupMembers

RT allows both users and groups to be members of groups. Because SQL databases don't generally provide a means to ask a database for all rows that refer to this row recursively, we have to build up a more complex mapping table.

Generally, everything you ever want to do with CachedGroupMembers is encapsulated in the interface to group objects. RT's CachedGroupMembers algorithm is quite complex and isn't designed to be modified by user code. Details of its schema are provided here for completeness.

CachedGroupMembers have the following fields:

MemberId
> As in the GroupMembers table, MemberId is a reference to the ID of a Principal that is a member of the group referenced by the GroupId.

Via
> In cases where a user or group is a member of a (parent) group, Via will point to the ID of the row in the CachedGroupMembers table for the parent group.
>
> When the group in question is the top-level group, Via points to this row's ID.[*]

ImmediateParentId
> ImmediateParentId is the ID of the Group that this row's MemberId is explicitly a member of. It corresponds directly to the GroupId in the GroupMembers table.

Disabled
> If this cached group member is a member of this group by way of a disabled group or if this group is disabled, this will be set to 1.
>
> This prevents us from finding members of disabled subgroups when listing off group members recursively. Also, it allows the access control system to elide members of disabled groups.

---

[*] To make the access control system work, it's important that a group be listed as a member of itself.

ACL

A single row in an access control list is an Access Control Entry or ACE. The Access Control List (ACL) table details which rights each Principal has for any ACLed object in RT. ACLed objects include: tickets, queues, and groups.

ACLs have the following fields:

PrincipalType
> PrincipalType captures which sort of object a given ACE applies to. For each of the roles—Owner, Requestor, Cc, and AdminCc—the PrincipalType is the name of that role.
>
> For regular groups, the PrincipalType is simply Group.
>
> For an ACE granting rights to a user, the PrincipalType is Group. Behind the scenes, rights are never granted directly to users, but to their ACL equivalence groups.

PrincipalId
> PrincipalId is a pointer to the principal to which this ACE applies. In the case of regular groups and role groups, it points to the group in question's Principal. If the ACE grants rights to a specific user, the PrincipalId points to that user's ACL equivalence group.

RightName
> The RightName is a simple textual identifier for the right being granted. For any object that supports access control, you can get a complete list of what rights it supports with the AvailableRights( ) method.

ObjectType
> Each ACE applies to a specific object. ObjectType is the class of that object. For example, if you granted a right on Queue 1, the class would be RT::Queue.

ObjectId
> ObjectId is the ID of the object to which this ACE refers. For example, if you granted a right on Queue 1, the ObjectId would be 1.

DelegatedFrom
> RT's ACL delegation system allows individual users to delegate rights that had been granted to them and automatically removes the delegated rights when the grantor's rights are revoked. DelegatedFrom is a pointer to the ID of the ACE on which this right is based.

DelegatedBy
> DelegatedBy is the Principal ID of the user who delegated this right.

Links

The Links table keeps track of relationships between entities. The object classes wrapping Links have built-in intelligence to do clever things with RT tickets, but you can think of the Links system as a simple store for RDF-style Subject-Predicate-Object triples (Base-Type-Target in RT's lexicon).[*]

Links have the following fields:

Base
> Base is the URI of the left-hand side of this link relation. It can contain any URI. By default, RT ships with classes that can handle *http:*, *https:*, *file:*, *ftp:* and *fsck.com-rt:* URIs.

LocalBase
> If this Link's base is a local ticket, LocalBase is a pointer to the ID of that ticket. This field is a convenience that makes it easier for RT to find links related to a particular ticket.

Type
> Type describes what sort of relationship the Base has to the Target. Out of the box, RT supports three simple types of relationships:

> *RefersTo*
>> The Base refers to the Target. This is a simple weak reference that lets you tie related objects together. For example, "The purchase of new servers *refers to* the estimates we got from these six vendors."

> *DependsOn*
>> The Base in some way depends on the Target. In the ticketing system side of RT, we use DependsOn to track cases when one Ticket must be completed before another one can be completed such as "The purchase of new servers *depends on* budget approval for the server migration project."

> *MemberOf*
>> The Target contains the Base. In the ticketing system side of RT, we use MemberOf to track parent-child relationships such as "The purchase of new servers is a *member of* the server migration project."

Target
> Target is the URI of the right-hand side of this link relation. It can contain any URI.

LocalTarget
> If this Link's target is a local ticket, LocalTarget is a pointer to the ID of that ticket. This field is a convenience that makes it easier for RT to find links related to a particular ticket.

---

[*] For more information about RDF, see *Practical RDF* (O'Reilly).

Attributes

RT's Attributes table, new in 3.2, allows you to store arbitrary metadata about any RT object. It's quite useful for extending objects in ways that we haven't envisioned. Bear in mind, though, that attributes aren't searchable. You can't for example, ask RT to find you all the Users who have an attribute called "LikesUnix."

ObjectType

>   ObjectType refers to what sort of RT object to which this attribute is attached. If you want to store an attribute for the user whose ID is 4, the attribute's Object-Type would be RT::User.

ObjectId

>   ObjectId is the ID of the object for which this attribute is being stored. If you want to store an attribute for the user whose ID is 4, the attribute's ObjectId would be 4.

Name

>   An attribute's Name is the machine-readable name for this attribute. RT uses attributes to store persistent searches. All saved searches have the name Saved-Search.

Description

>   An attribute's Description is the human readable explanation of the purpose of this particular attribute. For saved searches, this would be the user's hand-entered description for what's being searched.

Content

>   Content contains the actual value of this attribute. It can store at least 4,000 characters of text or binary data. Complex data structures are stored in the Perl "storable" format.

Transactions

Transactions record everything that happens to a ticket, from its creation through its eventual resolution. Each transaction can have one or more Attachments. Unlike most objects in RT, transactions are immutable once created.

Transactions have the following fields:

ObjectType

>   ObjectType describes the class of record to which this transaction refers. Most often, you'll see RT::Ticket here. (In previous versions, RT only tracked transactions on tickets). As of RT 3.4, RT also records changes to RT::User and RT::Group objects.

ObjectId

>   ObjectId is a pointer to the ID of the record to which this transaction refers.

Type

A transaction's Type describes what sort of update it is. For most simple updates to individual ticket fields, the type is Set. For adding a comment to a ticket, it's Comment. For updates to Custom Fields, it's CustomField.

TimeTaken

For some types of transactions, like Comment and Correspond, users can specify how long they spent on the update. TimeTaken tracks that value in minutes.

Field

For updates that alter a field or custom field, Field tracks what was changed.

OldValue

OldValue tracks what a field was changed *from*. In the case of deletion, OldValue is the value that was deleted.

NewValue

NewValue tracks what a field was changed *to*. In the case of a new value being added, NewValue tracks the new value.

Data

Some transactions have a bit more data than can be encapsulated easily in the previous fields. Data stores the subjects of incoming correspondence and occasionally other data.

ReferenceType

Some transactions store changes to custom fields for things like images, files, or large text blocks. When RT records one of those updates as a transaction, it sets ReferenceType to `RT::ObjectCustomFieldValue` and fills in OldReference and/or NewReference. Because storing two copies of these big objects can bloat the database, RT stores changes to large values like this by reference instead of just copying the values like it does for smaller fields.

NewReference

NewReference contains a pointer to an added value of the type stored in ReferenceType.

OldReference

OldReference contains a pointer to a deleted value of the type stored in ReferenceType.

Attachments

The Attachment table stores any message body or attachment for a transaction in a structured manner, so MIME email messages can be rebuilt.

Attachments are arbitrarily complex MIME entities that can be tied to tickets using transactions. Every email message that RT associates with a ticket will be stored in the database as one or more attachments. If an attachment is made up of multiple

MIME parts, RT will split those parts into a tree of related attachments and store each one in the database.

Attachments have the following fields:

TransactionId
> Each Attachment is associated with a Transaction. TransactionId is a reference to the ID of the Transaction associated with this attachment.

Parent
> If this attachment is part of a complex MIME structure, Parent points to another Attachment representing the parent MIME section.

MessageId
> If an attachment is an email message, MessageId stores its `Message-Id:` header. In the future, this will make it easier to build message threads.

Subject
> If an attachment is an email message, Subject stores its `Subject:` header.

Filename
> If an attachment is a named file, Filename stores what it was called when it was submitted to RT.

ContentType
> ContentType stores this attachment's MIME type.

ContentEncoding
> When possible, RT undoes all of the encoding that attachments are wrapped in for transport by email, so it can store them in their raw forms in the database. Some databases, like PostgreSQL and Oracle don't support binary data in the same sorts of fields that they use to store character data, like the bodies of email messages. On these databases, RT transparently encodes stored attachments into Base64 or QuotedPrintable encoding when stuffing them into the database and transparently undoes it when pulling them back out.
>
> Data about what sort of encoding is used is stored in the ContentEncoding header.

Content
> Content is the actual body of the attachment, stored as UTF-8 text, binary data, or encoded data.

Headers
> RT stores the attachment's message headers and MIME headers in the Headers field. RT also stores additional data, including the attachment's length and original text encoding, if it was converted into UTF-8 by RT.

CustomFields

RT allows sites to track custom metadata per ticket using a facility known as Custom Fields. These custom fields can be applied to tickets globally or per-queue. Custom fields can be of several types: *Select from a list, free-form data entry in a text field, free-form data entry in a textarea field* (with either plain or wiki text), *file upload*, and *image upload*. Additionally, each custom field can accept either *a single value* or *multiple values*. For all intents and purposes, users interacting with RT can treat custom fields the same as regular fields like Status and Subject. Users can see, edit, and search on custom field values through the same interfaces that they use to work with RT. At the API level, however, they're treated somewhat differently.

CustomFields have the following fields:

Name
> Each custom field has a name displayed to users editing or viewing it. Names aren't guaranteed to be unique.

Description
> Description is a human-readable summary of a custom field.

Type
> A custom field's Type describes what sort of values it accepts. As of RT 3.4, acceptable values are: Select, Freeform, Text, Image, and Binary. Select fields let the user pick values from a list. Freeform fields let the user enter individual lines of text. Text fields let the user enter large (up to a couple megabytes) blocks of text. Image fields let the user upload images as custom field values. Binary fields let the user attach files as values.

MaxValues
> MaxValues tells RT how many values this custom field can have for a given object. Out of the box, RT 3.4 lets users pick 0, which allows unlimited possible values, or 1, which limits users to a single selection.

SortOrder
> SortOrder is an integer field used by RT to automatically list custom fields in the order you want to present them. RT lists custom fields in ascending order sorted by SortOrder.

Disabled
> Disabled is a boolean field that specifies whether RT should let users see and modify a custom field and its values. It's important not to lose historical data about custom fields and their values, so disable custom fields instead of deleting them.

LookupType
> RT uses LookupType to describe what sorts of objects to which a custom field applies. `RT::Queue-RT::Ticket` means that the custom field applies to tickets in a given queue. `RT::Queue-RT::Ticket-RT::Transaction` means that the custom field

applies to transactions on tickets in a given queue. `RT::Group` tells RT that this custom field should apply to groups. Similarly, `RT::User` makes sure the custom field only shows up on user objects.

Pattern

RT 3.4 doesn't do anything with a custom field's Pattern attribute, but future releases or plugins will add the ability to validate users' input against a regular expression stored there.

Repeated

The Repeated attribute is reserved for future use.

CustomFieldValues

The CustomFieldValues table holds the list of acceptable values for Select custom fields.

CustomFieldValues have the following fields:

CustomField

CustomField is a pointer to the ID of the custom field for which this row holds a valid value.

Name

Name is the actual value of the custom field to be listed.

Description

Description is a longer explanation of the meaning of this value's Name. It's displayed in the administrative interface and some user-visible contexts.

SortOrder

SortOrder is an integer field used by RT to automatically list custom field values in the order you want to present them. Values fields are listed in ascending order.

ObjectCustomFields

ObjectCustomFields is a simple linking table that RT uses to decide which custom fields apply to a given object.

CustomField

CustomField is a reference to the ID of a record in the CustomFields table.

ObjectId

Using the custom field's LookupType, RT can figure out the type of objects to which the custom field can apply. ObjectId tells RT the exact object of that type to which a custom field applies. A value of 0 means that this custom field applies to all objects of that type.

ObjectCustomFieldValues

ObjectCustomFieldValues holds all current custom field values for all tickets within RT. Values are stored by value, rather than by reference. This enables users to switch custom field types from Select to Freeform and back again without loss of data.

CustomField
> CustomField is a pointer to the ID of the custom field associated with this value.

ObjectType
> ObjectType describes what sort of record to which this transaction refers. Its values are RT::Record subtypes. In RT, most transactions are on tickets, so the most common value you'll see is RT::Ticket, but others such as RT::Group and RT::User are also valid.

ObjectId
> ObjectId is a pointer to the ID of the record (usually a ticket) to which this value applies. In previous versions of RT, this column was called Ticket.

Content
> Content is the actual textual value of the custom field for the ticket. The content is stored as a 255 character text field.

LargeContent
> LargeContent stores larger text values for custom fields, as well as image or binary custom field values. As of RT 3.4, it's used by the Image, Text, and Binary custom field types.

ContentType
> ContentType stores the MIME type of any LargeContent. If there is no Large-Content for this record, it's blank. When searching custom field content, RT is careful to search only values that have a ContentType that begins with text.

ContentEncoding
> Because some databases handle binary data differently, ContentEncoding tells RT whether it needs to do anything special to decode and present the LargeContent.

Tickets

RT is a ticketing sytem. It should come as no suprise that one of the core objects is the Ticket. Every ticket has a number of things associated with it, including role groups for Owner, Requestors, Cc, and AdminCc. Owner is quite special in that it can contain only one user, but the others can contain multiple users and groups. By default, RT is configured to treat each of the groups specially, but internally they are quite similar. Additionally, a ticket can have a number of attached Transactions, CustomFields, and Links.

Tickets have the following fields:

EffectiveId

By default, a ticket's EffectiveId is the same as its ID. RT supports the ability to merge tickets together. When you merge a ticket into another one, RT sets the first ticket's EffectiveId to the second ticket's ID. RT uses this data to quickly look up which ticket you're really talking about when you reference a merged ticket.

Queue

Tickets are grouped into queues. Each ticket can have one and only one queue. Queue is a pointer to the ID of the queue for this ticket.

Type

Type is a simple textual identifer that describes what sort of ticket this is. By default, all tickets are of Type ticket. Generally, there's no reason to change that.

Owner

Owner is a pointer to the ID of the Principal who owns this ticket. This information is also stored in the ticket's Owner role group, but it is cached in the Ticket record for performance reasons.

Subject

Subject is a simple human-readable description of what this ticket is about.

Priority, InitialPriority, and FinalPriority

When a ticket is first created, its Priority is copied into its InitialPriority. An external tool can move a ticket's Priority up (or down) toward its FinalPriority.

TimeEstimated, TimeWorked, and TimeLeft

RT allows users to track how much time, in minutes, a given ticket is estimated to take. Over time, users can add to the TimeWorked and (hopefully) subtract from the TimeLeft.

Status

Each ticket has a single current Status, which can be one of new, open, stalled, resolved, rejected, or deleted. Deleted tickets are treated specially in that they can't be displayed in ticket listings.

Told

Told tracks the last time a ticket update was sent to the requestor.

Starts

Starts is primarily intended for users' project management needs. RT doesn't handle it specially.

Started

Started tracks the last time the ticket's status was flipped from new to another status.

Due

Due tracks the ticket's due date.

Resolved

The name Resolved is a bit misleading. This field tracks the last time that this ticket's status was set to resolved, rejected, or deleted.

IssueStatement and Resolution

These fields are not currently used by RT.

Queues

The Queue is RT's basic administrative unit. Every ticket is categorized into a Queue. Access control, business logic, notifications, and custom fields can all be configured at the queue level.

Queues have the following fields:

Name

Each queue has a unique Name. This name is displayed to users and used by tools such as RT's mail gateway to determine in which queue a new ticket should be created.

Description

Description is a human-readable explanation of a queue's purpose that is displayed to administrative staff and sometimes included in outgoing email messages about tickets in this queue.

CorrespondAddress

When RT sends out public email correspondence about a ticket, it automatically sets the message's From: and Reply-To: headers to the queue's CorrespondAddress. It's up to local staff to make sure that both this and the queue's CommentAddress are set to values that will be properly routed back into RT.

CommentAddress

When RT sends out private email comments about a ticket, it automatically sets the message's From: and Reply-To: headers to the queue's CommentAddress.

InitialPriority

InitialPriority specifies a default priority for a newly created ticket in this queue.

FinalPriority

FinalPriority specifies a default ending priority for a newly created ticket in this queue. RT ships with a small tool that you can insert into *cron* to automatically move tickets toward their FinalPriority as they approach their due dates.

DefaultDueIn

DefaultDueIn, if set, will set the due dates of newly created tickets in this queue to DefaultDueIn days in the future.

Disabled

Sometimes, you don't want a queue to appear in listings anymore. Deleting the queue outright would lose data about every ticket that had ever been in that queue. Instead, RT provides the Disabled flag, which simply masks the queues you don't want to see anymore.

Scrips

Scrips are one of RT's key bits of extensibility. Scrips are bits of custom logic that users can install into RT without changing any system code. Scrips are composed of a Condition and an Action. If the Condition returns success, then RT will prepare the Action. If the action is prepared cleanly, it is Committed and all relevant email is sent out and data written to the database.

Scrips have the following fields:

Description
> The Description is a simple human-readable explanation for this Scrip.

ScripCondition
> ScripCondition is a pointer to the ID of a ScripCondition object.

ScripAction
> ScripAction is a pointer to the ID of a ScripAction object.

CustomIsApplicableCode
> CustomIsApplicableCode is a field used primarily by user-defined conditions. Its content is used as the source code for an anonymous subroutine, which can return true or false. If it returns true, the Scrip's Action is prepared. Otherwise, processing of this scrip ceases.

CustomPrepareCode
> CustomPrepareCode is a field used primarily by user-defined actions. Its content is used as the source code for an anonymous subroutine, which can return true or false. If it returns true, the CustomCommitCode is evaluated. Otherwise, processing of this scrip ceases.

CustomCommitCode
> CustomCommitCode is a field used primarily by user-defined actions. Its content is used as the source code for an anonymous subroutine, which should perform whatever action the ScripAction needs to perform and return true on success or false on failure.

Stage
> Stages are the places in RT that call out to fire user-specified scrips. Valid values include:
>
> *TransactionCreate*
>> TransactionCreate is the standard scrip call-point from RT 2.0. Immediately after a transaction has been posted to the database, RT executes the scrip.

TransactionBatch

RT collects updates to a ticket into a single batch and executes all Transac-tionBatch scrips once the current `RT::Ticket` object has been marked for destruction.

Queue

Queue is the ID of the queue to which this scrip applies. If it's set to 0, this scrip applies to all queues.

Template

Template is a reference to the name of the template this scrip should use. If the template is a global template and there's a queue-specific template with the same name in this scrip's queue, RT will use the queue template.

ConditionRules and ActionRules

These fields are not currently used by RT.

Templates

Templates are simple text templates which Scrips use to build outgoing email messages. Their content is parsed with the `Text::Template` module.

Templates have the following fields:

Queue

Queue is a pointer to the ID of the queue with which this template is associated. If this template is a global template that should be available to scrips in all queues, Queue is 0.

Name

Name is a simple human-readable name for this template. Unlike most Names, it is sometimes used by RT to find templates.

Description

Description is a simple human-readable description for this template.

Content

Generally, a template's Content is an email message template that a Scrip interprets and sends off. RT uses a simple heuristic to determine whether a template's content contains email message headers; if the content's first line contains a colon (:), it's assumed to be a message header. RT treats each line as a header until it finds a blank line.

Type, Language, and TranslationOf

These fields are not used by RT.

ScripActions

ScripActions are references to chunks of code on disk, which are used by Scrips to perform some action. Examples include: *Autoreply to Requestor*, *Notify Owner*, and *Page Systems Administrators*.

ScripActions have the following fields:

Name
> Name is a simple human-readable name for this ScripAction. It's not used internally by RT.

Description
> Description is a longer human-readable description for this ScripAction. It's not used internally by RT.

ExecModule
> ExecModule is the name of the Perl module in *lib/RT/Action/* that should be called by this ScripAction. That Perl module must be a subclass of `RT::Action::Generic`.

Argument
> Argument contains an optional argument to be passed to the Action module during evaluation. RT's Notify ScripAction uses this argument to define which roles should receive mail from a particular scrip.

ScripConditions

ScripConditions are references to chunks of code on disk, which scrips use to perform some check or validation. Examples include: *On Create*, *On Correspond*, or *If the smoke alarm is going off*.

ScripConditions have the following fields:

Name
> Name is a simple human-readable name for this ScripAction. It's not used internally by RT.

Description
> Description is a longer human-readable description for this ScripAction. It's not used internally by RT.

ExecModule
> ExecModule is the name of the Perl module in *lib/RT/Action/* that should be called by this ScripAction. That Perl module must be a subclass of `RT::Condition::Generic`.

Argument
> Argument contains an optional argument to be passed to the Action module during evaluation. RT's "Notify" ScripAction uses this argument to define which roles should be receiving mail from a particular scrip.

ApplicableTransTypes

ApplicableTransTypes specifies a comma-delimited list of transaction types to which this ScripCondition applies. "Any" means that the ScripAction will run on any transaction. This serves as a first line of defense to cut down on the amount of processing that RT needs to do on any ticket update.

CHAPTER 9

API

In RT, the `DBIx::SearchBuilder` module is responsible for connecting to the database, building the SQL required—whether searching, creating, or editing data—and returning the data to the RT interface. It supplies the API (Application Programming Interface), which provides access to the data stored in the database and is an essential component of RT.

More than that, because this module has been built to execute SQL in a generic manner and to run against multiple different types of databases, your own programs also can use it. In this chapter we discuss `DBIx::SearchBuilder` in some detail, which will enable you to understand what it does behind the scenes for RT and how to leverage its functionality for your own nefarious purposes.

How It Works

`DBIx::SearchBuilder` is not supposed to be used directly for each record. It is designed to act as a base for other modules that add the appropriate behavior. Any application that uses the `DBIx::SearchBuilder` suite is likely to start by using the `DBIx::SearchBuilder::Record` modules as a wrapper for a particular object.

Because the easiest way to understand something is to use it, we'll write some simple code to interface with `DBIx::SearchBuilder`. Note that the code here is minimal so that you can concentrate on the interface. For more complex examples, simply browse the RT source code libraries themselves.

To show how this fits together, let's begin with a database handle, which every object needs if it wants to talk to the database.

DBIx::SearchBuilder::Handle

The first thing to do is to load the appropriate module.

```
use DBIx::SearchBuilder::Handle;
```

Followed by a call to its constructor:

```
my $handle = DBIx::SearchBuilder::Handle->new();
```

This is a generic database handle object that still needs to connect to a database before it can do anything useful. The Connect method connects to a database:

```
$handle->Connect(
        Driver          => 'mysql',
        Database        => 'dbname',
        Host            => 'hostname',
        User            => 'dbuser',
        Password        => 'dbpassword'
);
```

The following example is a simple command sent to an Oracle database to return and print the current date:

```
print $handle->FetchResult("SELECT sysdate FROM dual");

30-DEC-04
```

Although the $handle is a generic database handle, it is not a DBI handle. However, if you want to ping the database, or use any other standard DBI handle method, you can retrieve the DBI handle itself with the dbh method and use it directly:

```
$dbh = $handle->dbh;

die "Couldn't talk to the database" unless $dbh->ping;
```

DBIx::SearchBuilder::Record

To create some code to handle queries and retrieve data from the database, we need to write a small module wrapper around DBIx::SearchBuilder::Record. The following short chunk of code creates a small package called Tkt as a limited window on the tickets table in our database.

```
1 package Tkt;
2
3 use           DBIx::SearchBuilder::Handle;
4 use base qw(DBIx::SearchBuilder::Record);
5
6 sub _Init {
7     my $self    = shift;
8     my $handle = DBIx::SearchBuilder::Handle->new;
9     $handle->Connect(Driver => 'Oracle', User=>'rt', Password=>'rt');
10     $self->_Handle($handle);
11     $self->Table('Tickets');
12 }
13
14 sub _ClassAccessible {
15     {
16         Id      => { read => 1 },
17         Status  => { read => 1, write => 1 },
```

```
18          Subject => { read => 1 },
19     };
20 }
21
22 1;
```

First, we inherit all of `DBIx::SearchBuilder::Records` methods (line 4). The `_Init` subroutine creates the necessary database handle (line 8) and connects to the database (line 9). Next, the `Table` method registers the `Ticket` table as our data source (line 11). Finally the `_ClassAccessible` subroutine (line 14 to line 20) specifies certain fields and their access rights.

Using our new module is as simple as the following few lines of code:

```
1 use Tkt;
2
3 my $rec = Tkt->new;
4
5 $rec->Load(21);
6
7 printf("%s: %s (%s)\n", $rec->id, $rec->Subject, $rec->Status);
```

We instantiate the object (line 3), then query the database and load the complete record into it, identified by the unique ID 21 (line 5). At this point we simply print out the relevant fields (line 7) using the accessor methods from the `_ClassAccessible` subroutine we declared in our module earlier. The output displays the requested information:

```
21: My frobnitz is broken (open)
```

We also can update this record in the database using automatically created mutator methods. To change the status we pass the `SetStatus` method an appropriate argument (in this case `resolved`) and print the new values for reference. Repeating the command on line 7 prints out and confirms the change of status for our ticket:

```
8
9 $rec->SetStatus('resolved');
10
11 printf("%s: %s (%s)\n", $rec->id, $rec->Subject, $rec->Status);
12
```

The output displays the now modified information:

```
21: My frobnitz is broken (resolved)
```

Note that if you attempt to modify or write to a field that is not declared in the `_ClassAccessible` subroutine as `write => '1'`, the column is not updated and the method returns an appropriate "Immutable field" message. We should then print out the subject line to reassure ourselves of the true value of the field (line 14):

```
13 print "Update: ".$rec->SetSubject('a new subject line')."\n";
14
15 print "Subject: ".$rec->Subject."\n";
16
```

The current subject line for reference follows the failed output message:

```
Update: Immutable field
Subject: My frobnitz is broken
```

When we're working with the code, it might be nice to know what values are readable and writable, without having to search through the code for the relevant definitions. Fortunately DBIx::SearchBuilder::Record helps us out here, too, by providing a pair of handy methods that print out an array of the actual attributes for both cases. The following example demonstrates the ReadableAttributes method:

```
17 print "Readable attributes: ".join(', ', sort $rec->ReadableAttributes)."\n";
```

The output correctly prints out the readable attributes for this object.

```
Readable attributes: Id, Status, Subject
```

The following example is the matching WritableAttributes method:

```
18 print "Writable attributes: ".join(', ', sort $rec->WritableAttributes)."\n";
```

The output again confirms that the only field of this object that we may modify is the status field.

```
Writable attributes: Status
```

DBIx::SearchBuilder provides several other useful utility methods. One, called Table( ), prints out the name of the table where the object gets its data.

```
19 print "Table: ".$rec->Table."\n";
```

The output confirms the table name for our object.

```
Table: Tickets
```

Another useful method is PrimaryKeys( ). This helpfully tells us not only what the table's primary keys are called, but it also returns the values for the current object, if it has any.

```
20 print "Primary keys: ".join('=', $rec->PrimaryKeys)."\n";
```

The output confirms that we have a single primary key with a name of id, and that for the instance of the object which we are currently working with, it has the value of 21.

```
Primary keys: id=21
```

This API isn't only suitable for searching existing data records, it also creates and deletes them. When using the Create( ) method, the important thing to bear in mind is that you are responsible for checking the validity of the primary keys and any mandatory fields. Indeed, this is what RT itself handles when it wraps DBIx::SearchBuilder::Record methods.

First, we Create( ) an object with an appropriate primary key, and several attribute values.

```
21 $rec->Create(Id => 12345, subject=>'This is a new Ticket', status=>'fresh');
```

Next, we use the Load method we saw earlier to read this object cleanly from the database.

```
22 $rec->Load(12345);
```

Now we reuse the code from line 7 again, to print out the relevant values, and take a look at our new object.

```
23 printf("Ticket %s: %s (%s)\n", $rec->id, $rec->Subject, $rec->Status);
```

The resulting line confirms the new record was created satisfactorily.

```
Ticket 12345: This is a new Ticket (fresh)
```

The matching method is Delete( ) and is even simpler to use. It requires no arguments and simply deletes the current object from the database.

```
24 $rec->Delete;
```

Although this is a small example, you can see this is both simple and powerful. The code is generic and adaptable for many purposes. RT uses this flexibility to create a core of code that can manage a complicated application with consummate ease.

DBIx::SearchBuilder::Record offers a number of other useful methods. To read more about the available functionality that Tkt inherits, read the documentation for DBIx::SearchBuilder::Record.

DBIx::SearchBuilder

We've seen how to use DBIx::SearchBuilder::Record to work with a single record or object. A similar approach applies to collections of records. This section uses DBIx::SearchBuilder to handle many records at once.

The following code is a wrapper around DBIx::SearchBuilder. It is remarkably similar to the example in the previous section. The main differences are that we inherit from DBIx::SearchBuilder directly (line 4), and we use the Tkt class from the previous section to return each object from the database (line 17) in turn.

```
1 package Tkts;
2
3 use      Tkt;
4 use base qw(DBIx::SearchBuilder);
5
6 sub _Init {
7     my $self   = shift;
8     my $handle = DBIx::SearchBuilder::Handle->new;
9     $handle->Connect(Driver => 'Oracle', User=>'rt', Password=>'rt');
10     $self->_Handle($handle);
11     $self->Table('Tickets');
12     return ( $self->SUPER::_Init(Handle => $handle) );
13 }
14
15 sub NewItem {
16     my $self = shift;
```

```
17      return(Tkt->new);
18 }
19
20 1;
```

Now we use a short piece of code to get a handle (line 3) to define our search criteria (line 5). We print out the number of records found (line 7). Note that an alternative to using the Limit method is to use the UnLimit method, which returns all records.

```
1 use Tkts;
2
3 my $recs = Tkts->new;
4
5 $recs->Limit( FIELD => 'Subject', OPERATOR => 'LIKE', VALUE => '%urgent%');
6
7 print "Tickets: ".$recs->Count()."\n";
8
```

It prints something like:

```
Tickets: 5
```

At this point we loop through each object, printing out both the subject and status of each ticket to receive feedback on each issue. Note that each object returned from the Next() method is an object of the Tkt class. This means it is Loaded by DBIx::SearchBuilder and has all the power of a Tkt object available in the automatically created accessor and mutator methods described above.

```
9 while (my $rec = $recs->Next) {
10     printf("%s: %s (%s)\n", $rec->id, $rec->Subject, $rec->Status);
11 }
12
```

The output would look something like this:

```
81: an urgent contact request (new)
44: another very urgent issue (open)
45: urgent contact request (open)
22: an urgent problem (rejected)
61: extremely urgent disaster (new)
```

This is just skimming the surface of the DBIx::SearchBuilder's functionality. It has many other useful methods for working with record collections. Let's have a look at a couple that help to control the while loop shown above.

As you'd expect, calling the Next() method on our $recs collection object iterates through the list of objects returned from the database. What you may not expect is the handy feature that if you come to the end of the list—indicated by Next() returning undef which signals the end of the while loop—the following next Next() call starts at the first object again.

The next several lines of code use the object indirectly on the end of the print statement, rather than explicitly retrieving each object and then using it to print out one of its attributes. This saves paper, contributes to world peace, and makes a logical line of code all in one shot.

From the end of the `while` loop above, we simply print the Next( ) ID. Because we're starting at the beginning of the loop again, the ID should be 81.

```
13 print "ReStart loop Id: ".$recs->Next->id."\n";
14
```

```
ReStart loop Id: 81
```

Printing the next one produces the second object ID from our original list:

```
15 print "Next Id: ".$recs->Next->id."\n";
16
```

```
Next Id: 44
```

Simply iterating through the list in a round-robin fashion is probably the most common use of this sort of construct, but there's more. You also can go directly to any particular element of the current list using the GotoItem( ) method, passing it an integer to identify which item to go to.

Let's go directly to item 4 and print out the Next( ) ID. Item 4 has an ID of 22, and item 5 has an ID of 61:

```
17 $recs->GotoItem(4);
18
19 print "Fifth Id: ".$recs->Next->id."\n";
20
```

```
Fifth Id: 61
```

We also can go to the First( ) item in our list and print out its ID, which as we already know is 81:

```
21 print "First Id: ".$recs->First->id."\n";
22
```

```
First Id: 81
```

From looking at the list returned earlier, we can see that the Next( ) ID should be 44, but we're going to check this:

```
23 print "Next Id: ".$recs->Next->id."\n";
24
```

```
Next Id: 44
```

Want to know what the Last( ) ID was? Use the Last( ) method to retrieve that object.

```
25 print "Last Id: ".$recs->Last->id."\n";
26
```

```
Last Id: 61
```

Because DBIx::SearchBuilder uses data that it has stored internally, the working data may get out of sync with the actual data in the database while you iterate over various objects. As a demonstration, first instantiate a new Tkt object, then use the Create() method to store the record in the database:

```
27 my $newrec = new Tkt;
28
29 $newrec->Create(Id => 66, Subject => 'yet another urgent issue', queue => 1);
30
```

After you create the new record in the database, it is important to Load() the record into the object, otherwise you will be working with a bare Tkt object with no data.

```
31 $newrec->Load(66);
32
```

Now print out the familiar fields to check the results:

```
33 printf("%s: %s (%s)\n", $newrec->id, $newrec->Subject, $newrec->Status);
34
```

```
66: yet another urgent issue ()
```

Although the database knows there is an extra record in the table, DBIx:: SearchBuilder does not. Let's use the Count() method to see how many objects we have currently.

```
35 print "Current Count: ".$recs->Count."\n";
36
```

```
Current Count: 5
```

This count is correct for our current data but wrong from the perspective of the database. To get the true data collection, we need to use the CleanSlate() method and rerun our Limit() query.

```
37 $recs->CleanSlate;
38
39 $recs->Limit(FIELD => 'Subject', OPERATOR => 'LIKE', VALUE => '%urgent%');
40
```

Now we can take another look at our current count:

```
41 print "Updated Count: ".$recs->Count."\n";
42
```

```
Updated Count: 6
```

That looks much better. We also can use the handy ItemsArrayRef() method to return a reference to an array of all the items found by the search. Looping through this with a join() and a map(), we print out a list of all object IDs we have at our disposal to check that our 66 ID is actually in there, too.

```
43 print join(', ', map { $_->id } @{$recs->ItemsArrayRef})
44
```

```
81, 44, 66, 45, 22, 61
```

This last command deletes the object we created in this small run of code, both to demonstrate that the Delete( ) method works here too, and so that you can use this code repeatedly without violating unique database constraints for our extra object while testing.

```
45 $newrec->Delete;
46
```

DBIx::SearchBuilder offers a number of other useful methods. To read more about the functionality the Tkts object inherits, read the documentation for DBIx::SearchBuilder.

RT Codebase

RT's object-oriented code is arranged in several distinct groups of modules. Each group generally depends on a specific core or essential module that provides methods other modules can inherit or overload as appropriate: RT::Base, RT::Record, and RT::SearchBuilder.

RT::Base is a relatively minor but central utility module, which sets the current user for ACL decisions and the like. The following classes inherit this functionality:

```
RT::Date
RT::Record
RT::SearchBuilder
RT::System
RT::URI
```

RT::Record inherits from DBIx::SearchBuilder::Record and is responsible for handling a single object corresponding to a single record in the database. The following classes inherit from RT::Record:

```
RT::ACE
RT::Attachment
RT::Attribute
RT::CurrentUser
RT::CustomField
RT::Group
RT::GroupMember
RT::Link
RT::Principal
RT::Queue
RT::Scrip
RT::ScripAction
RT::ScripCondition
RT::Template
RT::Ticket
RT::Transaction
RT::User
```

RT::SearchBuilder also inherits from DBIx::SearchBuilder. It provides methods and functionality for collections of objects. The following collection objects inherit from RT::SearchBuilder:

```
RT::ACL
RT::Attachments
RT::Attributes
RT::CustomFields
RT::GroupMemebers
RT::Groups
RT::Links
RT::Principals
RT::Queues
RT::ScripActions
RT::ScripConditions
RT::Scrips
RT::Templates
RT::Tickets
RT::Transactions
RT::Users
```

You saw earlier that DBIx::SearchBuilder records and collections always take a database handle as a parameter to their _Init methods. The RT::Record and RT::SearchBuilder objects take care of this for you. But there's an added wrinkle. Within RT, every object needs to know which user is working with it so that it can make the right access control decisions and keep good records of who does what. With few exceptions, every RT object's new method takes only a single paremeter, an RT::CurrentUser object. (For bootstrapping reasons RT::CurrentUser can take a username or id number instead of an RT::CurrentUser object.) RT doesn't pass this information back to DBIx::SearchBuilder but uses it internally to make access control decisions.

RT implements ACLs (Access Control Lists) as the control mechanism for authorization for ticket and object creation. If you set the ACLs to permit the Everyone group to create tickets, RT automatically creates accounts for every user who ever submits a ticket. You can read more about ACLs and how RT uses them in Chapters 2 and 5.

Other modules are worth browsing to discover the functionality provided by the standard RT distribution. Action::Generic, Condition::Generic, Search::Generic, and URI::base are just a few ideas for further research and exploration. RT has a rich code base. Explore further to find your own ideas and solutions for your own particular application requirements.

Exceptions

Errors are handled by cancelling (or rolling back) the current transaction at the database level and sending the error to the current interface—whether that's the command-line interface, email, or the web frontend—and to *syslog*. The */etc/syslog.conf* configuration file can specify different responses to generate for the various RT errors and logging messages.

To get at the SQL, look at the relevant database logs. Alternatively you might try setting the DBI_TRACE variable to something suitably high to dump the SQL to STDERR.

Database Considerations

Because each database implements the SQL standard slightly differently, each database needs a slightly different schema for RT. One of the primary concerns is to ensure each object has a unique id field. To make things simple, RT handles the various compatability issues internally on your behalf. We can see how some of this is achieved by taking a look at several examples contained in the SQL that creates the Tickets table.

For MySQL, RT specifies an auto-incrementing id field directly within the CREATE TABLE statement. The Subject field takes a default value, and the Started field takes the current datetime if the value is NULL.

```
CREATE TABLE Tickets (
  id INTEGER NOT NULL AUTO_INCREMENT,
  Subject varchar(200) NULL DEFAULT '[no subject]' ,
   Started DATETIME NULL,
   ...
);
```

For Oracle, RT defines an automatically incrementing sequence at installation time and uses it when the RT::Record class creates a new object. The Subject field takes a default value, and the Started field must be filled in manually. Again the RT::Record class takes care of this for us internally.

```
CREATE TABLE Tickets (
  id NUMBER(11, 0),
  Subject VARCHAR2(200) DEFAULT '[no subject]',
  Started DATE,
   ...
);
```

As you can see, RT accommodates the vagaries of each database type. It not only ensures a unique identifying integer for the id field, but it also adapts the datatypes: VARCHAR2 for Oracle, VARCHAR for Informix, and so on. RT also accommodates Postgres, SQLite, and Sybase seamlessly.

Id

Because RT already has taken care of all these things internally, probably the most important thing to remember when making any changes to the default schema is to make sure it's always easy to determine the row in the database to which an object relates. DBIx::SearchBuilder expects every database table it works with to have a single auto-incrementing integer primary key called id. Other than that, you are more or less free to design your own schema or modify RTs, so long as the code reflects the tables you create.

Joins

Internally, RT generates its own SQL statements from the criteria specified in the various user interfaces and the currently excuting tasks.

Inner joins

Normally when RT joins one table to another table, the type of join generated is an inner join. This rejects rows that do not have a matching row in both tables—with an identical value in a particular (usually unique) column—as not satisfying the requirements of the query.

For example, you might ask RT to return a list of users and their tickets constrained by ticket status. In this case you would only want to see the users with tickets whose status matched to the criteria given.

Outer joins

Occasionally RT is required to perform a left (outer) join. This accepts records from the left-hand table even if they do not have matching rows in the right-hand table. In this case RT still returns the rows in the left-hand table with null rows (no data) for the right-hand table.

For example, you might ask RT to return a list of users and their tickets. Some users in the database might not have any tickets yet. You would still want to see the entire list of users, both those with tickets and those without tickets.

Transactions and Data Integrity

Transactions are handled on a per action basis. In other words, when a new ticket is created, all the elements that make up the new ticket are handled as a single transaction. For example, creating a ticket might involve the following actions:

1. Create a new ticket.
2. Create a new user if the user has not been seen before, and ACL controls allow anyone to create a new ticket.
3. Assign the ticket to an existing group (optional).
4. Assign the ticket to an existing queue (optional).

If any step along the way fails, the ticket is not created. You always have the opportunity to fix the errant behavior and to retry the transaction.

CHAPTER 10

Development Environments

We've already seen some examples of how you can modify RT's behavior through custom scrips, templates, and actions, but RT can be customized even further. You also may need to work on RT's core code, either to develop features to submit back to the core developers or to fix bugs that you find.

DevelMode

Enabling RT's development allows several features that make developing RT and RT extensions much simpler. There are several ways you can do this. You can enable RT's "developer mode" feature when running the *configure* script by adding the --with-devel-mode switch.

You also can edit the *etc/RT_SiteConfig.pm* file to include this line:

```
Set($DevelMode => 1);
```

The --with-devel-mode configuration option simply adds this line to the *etc/RT_Config.pm* file.

Turning on development mode disables the static_source and use_object_files Mason features, which means that components are re-parsed for every request. This guarantees that changes to components will be seen immediately.

It also enables the use of Module::Refresh, which checks for changes to modules on each new request. Without this, it would be necessary to restart the HTTP server every time a module was changed.

Modifying RT's Codebase

Most of RT's core classes are designed to allow you to customize their behavior through a mechanism called *overlays*. You also can use subclasses in some cases, or modules such as Damian Conway's Hook::LexWrap.

Overlays

Overlays are the easiest way to make major changes to RT's core classes. If you look at the RT::User class itself, you will see that it contains surprisingly little code.

Near the end, you'll see these lines:

```
eval "require RT::User_Overlay";
if ($@ && $@ !~ qr{^Can't locate RT/User_Overlay.pm}) {
    die $@;
}

eval "require RT::User_Vendor";
if ($@ && $@ !~ qr{^Can't locate RT/User_Vendor.pm}) {
    die $@;
}

eval "require RT::User_Local";
if ($@ && $@ !~ qr{^Can't locate RT/User_Local.pm}) {
    die $@;
}
```

This is the core of RT's overlay mechanism. The RT::User_Overlay file ships with RT itself and contains most of the real core logic for the user class. It is important to note that this module's package declaration is RT::User.

The RT::User_Vendor module would be created by an operating system distribution like Debian or FreeBSD, and the RT::User_Local module is where per-installation custom code should be placed. Neither of these modules exist in a default RT installation.

This mechanism is somewhat unusual, and you may wonder why RT doesn't just use subclasses. The first reason is that many of RT's core database-based classes are auto-generated from the database schema. Additionally, using subclasses would require all classes that use RT::User (for example) to use the appropriate subclass instead, which requires a potentially complex configuration mechanism and could be a bit of a headache.

The downside is that you cannot use SUPER to call the code you've overridden. If you need to do that, you will need to use Hook::LexWrap, or assign another name to the original subroutine:

```
BEGIN { *SUPER_SomeMethod = \&SomeMethod };

sub SomeMethod {
    my $self = shift;
    # ...some preprocessing...
    $self->SUPER_SomeMethod(@_);
    # ...some postprocessing...
}
```

Quieting warnings

Let's assume that you've created a module RT::User_Local, and you've overridden the CurrentUserHasRight( ) method. When you go to restart RT, you'll get a warning like "Subroutine CurrentUserHasRight redefined at ... RT/User_Local.pm line 42."

This is not a helpful warning, since you already know you redefined that subroutine. You can silence it by adding this line to the top of your module:

```
no warnings 'redefine';
```

A simple overlay example

In a default RT setup, all of the user data is stored in RT's database. But what if you want to get some of the user data from another source, like an LDAP directory or a different database? The answer is to create a User_Local.pm overlay module.

Here is a simple example that overrides the CanonicalizeUserInfo( ) method to lookup the user's real name using an in-house module:

```
package RT::User;

use strict;
no warnings 'redefine';

use Yoyodyne::User;

sub CanonicalizeUserInfo {
    my $self = shift;
    my $args = shift;

    my $user = Yoyodyne::User->new( $args->{EmailAddress} );

    $args->{RealName} = $user->name
        if $user;

    return 1;
}

1;
```

This method, CanonicalizeUserInfo( ), does nothing in the core RT classes and is explicitly provided to make it easy to customize user creation.

Hook::LexWrap

You can use the Hook::LexWrap module to achieve something similar to overriding a method in a subclass. Hook::LexWrap lets you insert pre- and post-call wrappers for a method or function call. Code run before the method can change the arguments being passed in, and code run after can change the return value.

Hook::LexWrap calls the wrapper code with an extra argument at the end of @_. If you set this value in your pre-call code, then the main method and post-call code will not be called. You can use this to short-circuit a method call and force a different return value.

Here's an example that takes advantage of that to prevent the resolution of a ticket which has never had a reply:

```
package RT::Ticket;

use strict;
use Hook::LexWrap;

wrap 'SetStatus' => pre => \&check_for_replies;

sub check_for_replies {
    my $self = shift;

    my $transactions = RT::Transactions->new( $self->CurrentUser );
    $transactions->LimitToTicket( $self->Id );
    $transactions->Limit( FIELD => 'Type',
                          VALUE => 'Correspond',
                        );

    unless ( $transactions->Count ) {
        $_[-1] = [0, $self->loc('Ticket cannot be resolved without a reply')];
    }
}

1;
```

This code would go in *local/lib/RT/Ticket_Local.pm*.

The wrapper code short-circuits the call to SetStatus( ) if the ticket has no replies. This is done simply by setting the value of the last argument to the wrapper. If this argument is an array reference, then Hook::LexWrap will turn it into an array if the original method was called in array context.

If the ticket has replies, then the wrapper does not set this value, so the original method is called in the normal fashion.

Access Control

When adding new functionality to RT, you may need to implement access controls. RT has an access control system that you can use in your extensions. You also can add new rights to the system if necessary.

To check that a user has a specific right, simply call HasRight( ) on that user object. This method is usually called with two arguments, Right and Object. Right is simply the name of the right to be checked, such as SuperUser or ModifyTicket. Object is the object the user is trying to access. The method will return a boolean indicating whether the user has the given right.

For example, if we have a queue and want to see if the user can see that queue, we call:

```
$user->HasRight( Right => 'SeeQueue', Object => $queue );
```

Many classes define a convenience method called `CurrentUserHasRight()`, which simply takes a single unnamed argument, the name of the right. So if we want to know if the current user has the "SeeQueue" right, we call:

```
$queue->CurrentUserHasRight('SeeQueue');
```

Some classes define other rights-related convenience methods. See the POD documentation for individual classes for more details.

Adding a new right

Currently, rights are defined simply as a global hash reference in `RT::Group_Overlay`, `RT::Queue_Overlay`, and `RT::CustomField_Overlay`. To add a new right, you can use this boilerplate in the appropriate *_Local.pm* module:

```
$RIGHTS = {
    SeeDeadPeople => "members of this group are allowed to see dead people",
    %$RIGHTS,
};
```

Since the local overlay is always loaded last, it is safe to assume that `$RIGHTS` was populated already by the RT core code.

Profiling

Profiling RT code is simple if you use the standalone HTTP server that comes with RT. [*] Profiling requires the following steps:

1. Start the standlone HTTP server with the Perl profiling flag (-d:DProf).

2. Run many requests that exercise the same code. This is necessary in order to ensure that the cost of simply starting up the server does not outweigh the cost of the code you want to profile.

3. Exit cleanly, do not just abort the HTTP server process. This makes sure that the state of the Perl interpreter does not become corrupted.

The last step requires that we add a simple extra top-level Mason component, which we will call *exit.html*. Place this in *local/html* under your RT installation directory. The component should look like this:

```
% exit;
```

---

[*] Here we cover only profiling module code in *lib/*. To profile Mason components, use the `MasonX::Profiler` module, which is available on CPAN.

Of course, this is not something you want in a production installation, since it would let anyone abort a process with a simple HTTP request.

To start the standalone server with profiling turned on, run it as, */path/to/perl -d: DProf /path/to/standlone_httpd*.

Then run the same request many times. To exit, simply call the exit.html component, which should be available via a URL of */exit.html*.

When the process exits, the Perl profiler leaves behind a file *tmon.out*. Use the dprofpp script to see the results of the profiling in various formats.

If you have RT's development mode turned on, you may want to turn it off when profiling, as development mode adds non-trivial overhead to each request that is not present in a production environment.

Debugging

While it's always nice when your code runs perfectly the first time you use it, you probably will have to spend some time debugging your RT extensions.

Debugging web applications can be tricky. If you can write a standalone script to exercise a piece of code, you can use Perl's debugger. Run perldoc perldebug for details.

If your code is dependent on being run in the web environment, then you cannot use the debugger.

RT's Logging System

You can use RT's own logging system in your extensions, which is useful for debugging. RT uses Log::Dispatch from CPAN to implement debugging. This module has a very simple API for logging messages. You simply call a method name matching the log level you want to use, and pass it a message:

```
$RT::Logger->debug("entering bake_cake method");

$RT::Logger->critical("cannot contact the mothership!");
```

RT configures Log::Dispatch to add additional information to your message, including a timestamp and the file and line number where the message was generated. Logging can be configured in the *etc/RT_SiteConfig.pm* file to go to the screen, a file, or to use syslog.

For development, you should configure at least one of the log outputs to run at the "debug" level, which is the lowest posssible level, ensuring that you see all the messages that are generated.

RT's Test Infrastructure

RT has a test infrastructure that you should use if you are doing core RT development. This helps ensure that any changes you make do not break existing functionality and adding tests for bug fixes or new features makes it easier for RT's core developers to integrate patches.

Running the Test Suite

There are two *make* targets that can run regression tests. Running the tests installs RT to whatever location was specified when *configure* was run. You may want to run *configure* with --enable-layout=inplace, which will make RT simply use the files in the current location.

The regression target will use *apachectl* to start and stop the Apache server for some tests. It assumes that whatever *apachectl* it is configured to use controls a server that is configured to run RT. The regression-noapache target will start the standalone HTTP server on port 80 to run tests against.

Interpreting the Output

The tests use the standard Perl test harness. Tests are written in standard Perl and grouped into test files. As each test file runs, it prints a message showing the status of that file:

```
lib/t/autogen/autogen-RT-GroupMembers_Overlay............ok
```

This means that all the tests in this file ran correctly. If there are errors, these will be printed separately.

When all the tests have finished running, there will be a summary:

```
Failed Test                     Stat Wstat Total Fail  Failed  List of Failed
-------------------------------------------------------------------------------
lib/t/regression/02basic_web.t   255 65280     1    0   0.00%  ??
lib/t/regression/03web_compiliati 255 65280     1    0   0.00%  ??
lib/t/regression/06mailgateway.t  15  3840    40   15  37.50%  4 7 9 16 18-19
                                                              21 25-26 28
                                                              32-33 35 38 40
lib/t/regression/08web_cf_access.  3   768     4    3  75.00%  2-4
lib/t/regression/19-rtname.t     255 65280     1    0   0.00%  ??
```

This shows which test files had problems and which tests failed. If the list of failed tests is simply ??, that means that the test file probably died before generating any output.

Running an individual test file

If you want to run a specific file, you can use the *prove* utility that comes with recent versions of the Test::Harness module. Before running tests, you should clean out the test database by running make regression-reset-db. Then you can use prove to run a single file:

```
prove -Ilib -v lib/t/setup_regression.t lib/t/regression/19-rtname.t
```

The -Ilib switch adds *lib* to Perl's library path. You should change this to the appropriate location. The -v switch turns on verbose output. This is helpful for fixing individual test failures. The first test, *lib/t/setup_regression.t*, ensures that the environment is ready for further regression tests. This should always be run before any other individual tests. After that, simply put the path(s) of the test file(s) you want to run.

Tests Extracted from Modules

If you look inside an RT core module like *lib/RT/User_Overlay.pm*, you will notice sections like this:

```
=begin testing

ok(require RT::User);

=end testing
```

Code inside this block will be extracted and turned into a test file when you run make regression. This is done with the testify-pods make action, which can be run separately. If you are working on the RT core code, you are encouraged to add tests to these blocks. Ideally, there should be one test block per method, though not all methods currently have tests.

Tests extracted from modules all share a single lexical scope, so a test that occurs later in the file can refer to variables created previously.

The tests are extracted into *lib/t/autogen*, one file per module.

Writing Tests

When writing tests, you can use any of the testing functions provided by Test::More, as this is automatically loaded in each auto-generated test file. If you want to use other testing modules, you will need to load them explicitly.

What is a good test?

This is a big topic, and there are a lot of good books on testing that cover the topic in great depth. Here are some quick guidelines:

- Test one thing at a time, which means test one method with one set of arguments at once.
- Remember to test both success and failure conditions. If code should *fail* on certain inputs, make sure that it does so.

- It's probably better to have too many tests rather than too few. Some redundancy in testing is not a bad thing, and it may even turn up odd bugs, for example a method that fails after being called several times because of changes in an object's internal state.

Internationalization

RT can be configured to run in a variety of languages and has a lot of support internally for internationalization.

How RT's I18N Framework Works

Most of the text generated by RT is localized, except for log messages. Depending on what type of code you are writing, there are a few different ways to access RT's localization functions.

Inside a module—such as a script condition or overlay—RT offers the methods `loc( )` and `loc_fuzzy( )`.

Inside Mason components, there is a globally available function `loc( )` which does the same thing. If you want to localize a piece of inline text inside a component, you can wrap it in a filtering component call, like this:

```
<&|/l>My text</&>
```

This calls a Mason component that runs your text through an I18N filter and outputs the result.

Writing Internationalized Code

Whenever you generate a piece of text to be presented to the end user, you should use RT's I18N framework. Under the hood, RT uses `Locale::Maketext` and `Locale::Maketext::Lexicon` to implement I18N.

Bracket notation

To specify the string to localize, `Locale::Maketext` uses *bracket notation*, which is a mini-templating system. When localizing a string, you often need to interpolate variables. For example, if you want to localize "Found 6 tickets," you want to make the number of tickets found a variable. In bracket notation that would be `Found [*,_1,ticket]`. This tells the I18N system that the first parameter is some quantity of tickets. This allows it to properly pluralize "ticket." The first part of the notation, `*`, is shorthand for the quant method in `Locale::Maketext`.

Complete documentation of this notation can be found in the documentation for `Locale::Maketext`, and there are plenty of examples of its usage in the RT core code.

Localizing RT

Each localization of RT is contained in a single *.po* file installed under *lib/RT/I18N*. These files simply contain pairs of strings as found in the source, and their translated versions. For example, in the French translation, *fr.po*, we can see:

```
#: lib/RT/Group_Overlay.pm:1160
msgid "Group has no such member"
msgstr "Un tel membre n'appartient pas au groupe"
```

The `msgid` is what is passed in the call to the localization method, and the `msgstr` is the translated version.

RT comes with a utility to generate an empty message catalog for a new translation. Simply run the script *extract-message-catalog* from the root of your RT installation and give it the filename for the new catalog you would like created.

The new catalog will create a new empty catalog, along with comments indicating where each `msgid` comes from, as in the above example.

This script is not installed in a normal RT installation, but it is available from the source tarball.

RT Community

RT has an active community, including folks working on extending RT. If you want to participate, the best places to start are the RT wiki at *http://wiki.bestpractical.com/* and the RT email lists. See *http://www.bestpractical.com/rt/lists.html* for more information on the RT email lists.

If you have a question about developing an RT extension, the rt-devel list is the best place to ask.

Reporting Bugs

Before reporting a bug, please check the current bug list at *http://rt3.fsck.com/ NoAuth/Buglist.html* first. Bug reports should be sent to *rt-bugs@bestpractical.com*.

Patching RT

If you want to submit a patch to RT that makes major changes or adds a new feature, it is best to discuss it on the rt-devel list first. Patches for small bug fixes can be sent directly to *rt-bugs@fsck.com* along with the bug report.

Packaging and Releasing an RT Extension

If you've created an extension that you think would be generally useful for the RT community, you can package it and distribute it as a Perl module on CPAN, the Comprehensive Perl Archive Network.

All RT extensions placed on the CPAN should have a name starting with RTx to distinguish them from core RT code.

Module::Install::RTx

You can use Module::Install::RTx to help create an installer for your extension. It automates a number of RT-specific installation tasks, such as installing *.po* files for I18N, installing Mason components, and updating the database.

Here is an example *Makefile.PL* for a fictional RTx::MechaRepair extension:

```
use inc::Module::Install;

RTx('MechaRepair');
author('Dave Rolsky <dave@example.com>');
license('perl');

WriteAll();
```

Module::Install::RTx looks for certain directories in the distribution like *html* or *po* and makes sure that files in there end up in the appropriate place when installed. See the Module::Install::RTx documentation for details.

Updating the database

You can include SQL files to update the database under *etc/*. To change the database schema, use a file named *schema.XXX*, where XXX is the name of a DBI driver like "Pg" or "mysql." SQL to update ACLs should be named *acl.XXX*. If you have a file named *initialdata*, this can be used to run a set of INSERT or UPDATE statements to update the database.

If any of these files are present, the end user installing your extension will be able to run make initdb, which takes care of running *rt-setup-database* appropriately.

Licensing

RT is open source software, which is made freely available under the terms of version 2 of the GNU GPL. When you release an extension, we encourage you to use an OSI-approved license that is compatible with RT's. If you have any questions about appropriate licensing for your RT extensions, we encourage you to consult legal counsel.

Glossary

Like all technologies, RT has its own lingo, and understanding RT begins with understanding this lingo. RT began life as a help desk application, and much of the terminology reflects this fact. Over time, as RT developed unique features, it accumulated new terms. This appendix gives detailed explanations of a few common terms and their relationships to each other.

RT addons such as RTFM (RT FAQ Manager) and RTIR (RT for Incident Response) have their own lingo, which is not covered here. These products include their own documentation.

Ticket

The *ticket* is RT's primary object, and everything that is managed by RT is contained in a ticket. A ticket represents a request, bug report, incident, work order, project, lunch order, or whatever you're tracking with RT. As a user, most of your activity is ultimately about manipulating tickets. A ticket is identified by number and has a set of attributes, such as the subject or summary, who opened it, when it was opened, the priority of the request, and the current status. Some of these values will change over the lifespan of the ticket, such as the status, while some, such as the date the ticket was originally created, can't be altered.

Subject

The subject of a ticket is analogous to the subject of an email: a short summary of what the ticket is about, at most a few hundred characters, intended to convey the gist of the ticket at a casual glance. Since all search result displays include the subject, it is very important that the subject be concise.

Status

A ticket's status describes its current work state. There are several choices for classifying each ticket:

New
> The ticket has just been created and hasn't been touched yet.

Open
> The ticket is being worked on.

Stalled
> Due to circumstances beyond your control (waiting for the requestor to respond, waiting for the owner to return from Sri Lanka), the ticket isn't getting worked on right now. It will open again when someone adds a comment or reply.

Resolved
> Hooray! Work on the ticket has been completed and is out of everyone's hair.

Rejected
> The ticket is not the staff's problem and is not going to be resolved, but is, for some reason, worth recording in the system. For instance, if an employee asks approval for something ridiculous, you can reject the ticket, but it will stay in the database as evidence that the employee makes silly requests.

Deleted
> The ticket never should have been in the system—it was spam, it was a list of passwords, it was porn, use your imagination—and is now being zapped for good.

It is not unusual for the status to change several times, from new to open to resolved, bouncing between open and stalled a few times.

Body

The ticket's body is the full, detailed explanation of the ticket. It is maintained as a series of discrete elements, called *attachments*, which are grouped together in a *transaction*. A ticket's body consists of all its transactions, arranged chronologically.

Transaction

A transaction represents a single modification to a ticket, from status changes to adding content to the body. A transaction that adds content to the body of a ticket consists of one or more attachments. For example, if a user attaches a spreadsheet, or a screenshot, to a ticket, these become part of the ticket as a single transaction consisting of multiple attachments. Transactions that don't modify the body of the ticket, like attribute changes, do not have associated attachments.

Attachment

An attachment is a discrete piece of content added to the ticket body. RT borrows the concept of attachments from email (actually, from MIME). Every attachment is associated with a transaction. Like a ticket, an attachment has several attributes, including subject, content type, encoding, and a unique identifier.

Watchers

A watcher is someone who is interested in a ticket. Watchers are notified when something about the ticket changes. Some types of watchers are inherited from the queue in which the ticket lives, while others are attached to the ticket itself. There are several types of watchers:

Owner
> The person responsible for the ticket and its resolution. Each ticket can have only one owner at any given time.

Requestor
> The person or people who created the ticket or have a vested interest in the outcome.

Cc
> Someone who should get copies of any replies that go to the requestor. This might be the requestor's boss, sales rep, etc. This person will see the email but doesn't necessarily have the right to work on the ticket.

AdminCc
> A Cc that also gets copies of private comments about the ticket and generally has permission to work on the ticket.

People often find the distinction between Cc and AdminCc confusing. Basically, Cc means the same thing in RT as it does in email (someone that simply receives copies of correspondence), while AdminCc is RT-specific and indicates someone who can work on the ticket. In practice, though, the difference is not too important, and permissions can be applied to either type of watcher so that it can fill almost any role.

History

A ticket's history is what it sounds like: everything that has happened to a ticket. RT automatically tracks every change to a ticket, including when the ticket was created, how it has changed, and any comments about it or replies to it. Like real history, ticket history cannot be changed, so be aware that any comments you make about a ticket are permanent. This audit trail provides detailed information about not only what changed, but when it changed and who changed it. As of RT 3.4, RT also tracks every outgoing email about a ticket, so you can be sure that your boss really **was** notified that you submitted a vacation request.

Ticket updates can take one of two forms: *replies* and *comments*. A reply is a public remark that is sent to the requestor. A comment is a private note for staff that is not visible to the requestor. This is useful when you want to be tactful but still convey important information, like, "This requestor is an investor, so be nice" or "This user's request mentioned his 'PC' but he really has a Mac."

Priority

Priority represents the relative importance of a ticket. It is stored as a number from 0 to 99, with 99 generally being the highest priority. The difference between 25, 50, and 75 may vary from organization to organization, but there should be an organizational policy, or every ticket will get rated 99 by anxious users.

In addition to priority, a ticket can have an *initial priority* or a *final priority*. By setting either of these values, you can make a ticket's priority increase or decrease as its due date draws closer. Thus, the priority of a ticket is its current priority, which may or may not be equal to the initial or final priority.

Relationships

RT maintains *relationships* between tickets and other objects. Relationships in RT can be between multiple tickets on the same RT instance but also can link tickets to external items like URLs, FedEx shipping numbers, or even other bug tracking systems like Bugzilla. RT defines a few basic types of relationships:

Depends on
> The ticket can't be resolved unless another ticket is also resolved. The converse is Depended on by.

Refers to
> The ticket doesn't need the other ticket, but it would sure be useful for you to look at it. The converse is Referred to by.

Parent
> A big, general ticket ("Move house").

Child
> A subproject of a parent ("Hire movers" "Pack" "Eat pizza").

By defining relationships between tickets, it is possible to clearly define a hierarchy of work that needs to be done in order for a ticket to be resolved. This can be helpful in figuring out dependencies; for example, if new feature X can't be added until bug Y is fixed, then the ticket for feature X depends on the ticket for bug Y and can't be resolved until the bug is fixed.

Dates

There are many dates associated with each ticket, everything from when the ticket was originally created, to when it was last modified, to when it was resolved. The system automatically sets some of these at the time of certain actions, while some can be modified by anyone with the appropriate rights.

Created
> The date that the ticket was initially created.

Starts
> The date when work should begin on the ticket. This field is set at ticket creation time.

Due
> The date by which the ticket should be completed. This field is set at ticket creation time.

Started
> The date that work was actually started on the ticket.

Last Contacted
> This date indicates that last time notification about the ticket was sent out. This field is sometimes known as Told.

Last Updated
> The date of the last modification to the ticket.

Resolved
> The date that the ticket was resolved. Obviously, this will be set only for resolved tickets.

The Created, Last Contacted, Last Updated, and Resolved dates are maintained by RT itself everytime the ticket is modified. Starts and Due can be set by anyone with permissions to modify the ticket.

Custom Fields

Custom fields (also known as CFs) are application-specific metadata that are created specifically for the local RT installation.

Starting with RT 3.4, custom fields can be applied to tickets, transactions on tickets, users, and groups. Each custom field can apply to only one type of object. Ticket and transaction custom fields can be tied to any number of queues, but user and group custom fields apply system-wide.

Custom fields can be one of several types:

Select
> A *Select* field has a predetermined set of values. For example, a CF containing a list of computer operating systems supported by the Help Desk would very likely be a *Select* CF.

Freeform
> *Freeform* fields contain single lines of text.

Text
> *Text* fields hold multi-line blocks of plain text.

Wikitext
> *Text* fields hold multi-line blocks of wiki text.

Binary
> *Binary* fields are uploaded files.

Image
> *Image* fields are like *Binary* files, but they are displayed on the Web UI instead of presented as download links.

In addition to its type, a custom field also has a *MaxValue* setting that limits the number of its entries. As of this writing, the web configuration interface only allows 1 (*Single* fields) and 0 (*Multiple* fields).

Queue

Disorganized tickets are hard to manage, so RT provides a container for grouping tickets: the *queue*. The queue is the central administrative domain of RT. As the name implies, it's a line of tickets waiting to be worked on, but it's also the ticket's category. Permissions are applied to queues, rather than directly to tickets, so which actions you can take on a ticket depends on the ticket's queue. For instance, you might have the right to create, delete, and comment on tickets in the Foo queue but only the right to comment on tickets in the Bar queue.

Scrip

Scrips are custom actions that are automatically triggered in response to specific conditions. The scrip machinery is very generalized and flexible, and it is able to do anything you can code in or call from Perl (i.e., just about anything at all). For example, you could have RT email the requestor when a ticket is resolved, send you an instant message when your boss submits a request, or mail ticket statistics to you when a ticket is closed. RT's default actions, such as sending mail on the creation of a new ticket, are handled by scrips. RT can apply scrips to all tickets or to all tickets in a specific queue. See Chapter 6 for more examples on using scrips.

Conditions

How does RT know whether to execute a scrip? This decision is based on the scrip's *condition*, which determines whether a scrip is applicable to the current transaction.

Templates

When a scrip is activated, it executes a *template*. Most templates turn into email messages, using the Text::Template module, but since you can embed Perl in them, they can do just about anything.

Users

A *user* represents a single entity within RT. Usually, the RT administrator creates users manually, but RT can be configured to autocreate user objects under certain conditions, such as when it receives mail from an email address that it has not seen before. Once a user exists, they can log in and modify their contact information, such as address, phone number, and preferred language.

Groups

Users are arranged into *groups*, which represent collections of users. Groups can be arranged in any way: following the corporate organization chart, to reflect which parts of the infrastructure they are responsible for, or even alphabetically. Users can be members of any number of groups, so groups can be used to organize users as well as configure access permissions.

There are several built in pseudo-groups, such as *Everyone* and *Owner*, which are defined under certain circumstances. These pseudo-groups are symbolic, and let the RT administrator assign special rights to users who have a specific relationship to a ticket. For example, the Owner pseudo-group might be the only one with the rights to close a ticket. Because the owner of a ticket might change over time, using this pseudo-group saves the administrator from having to write custom scrips to allow ticket resolution.

Principals

A *principal* is an entity capable of having access control applied to it, such as a user or group. Groups in RT must consist of principals, which means that a group can contain other groups, in addition to containing users. This allows the RT administrator fine-grained and flexible control over users.

ACL

RT has a rich authorization schema, based on Access Control Lists (ACLs). ACLs provide fine-grained control over what a user can and cannot do at the ticket, queue, group, and global levels. Rights can be granted by an administrator to specific users, groups, or *roles*—such as requestor, owner, or admin cc at the ticket—in which case what a user is allowed to do is a combination of user, group, and role ACLs. Access control is covered in more detail in Chapter 5, "Administration and Customization."

ACE

An *ACE* is an access control entry and represents a single right within RT's ACL system. Generally, ACEs are referred to by the specific right name, such as *CreateTicket*, *TakeTicket*, or *Watch*.

Command-Line Action Reference

The CLI has five basic actions—list, show, create, edit, and comment/correspond—and a number of subactions. The basic actions can operate on any object type, from tickets to queues to users, and most take options that modify the actions' behavior. The syntax for *rt* is essentially:

    rt *action* [*options*] [*arguments*]

An *action* is mandatory, an *option* is clearly optional, and most actions take *arguments*. For example, it makes sense for a list command to take at least one object ID as an argument. With some actions the arguments might be a list of field=value pairs to set.

---

create

rt create [*options*] set *field=value* [*field=value*] ...

The create action creates a new user or ticket. It has the same syntax and options as edit, except that create won't allow you to specify an object ID. See the section on edit below for the full set of options. The new action is another name for create.

rt new [*options*] set *field=value* [*field=value*] ...

---

edit

rt edit [*options*] *object-ids* set *field=value* [*field=value*] ...

                                        add *field=value* [*field=value*] ...

                                        del *field=value* [*field=value*] ...

The edit action modifies the information for one or more objects. The ed action is another name for edit. It typically starts an editor enabling you to edit object data in a plain-text form. With the create action the form is mostly filled with default or blank values. Once the form is written and closed, *rt* modifies or creates the object, as appropriate. The $EDITOR environment variable selects which editor rt will use; it defaults to vi.

If the command line passes enough information, *rt* submits the form directly to the RT server without any further interaction. The -e option guarantees you get the interactive editor no matter what you pass on the command line.

The edit and create actions have several options:

-

> Read object IDs from STDIN instead of the command line. Object IDs are not simply the id but the combination of object type and the object id:
>
>> ticket/42

-t *type*
> Specifies one of the valid RT object types: ticket, user, group, queue. This option also takes the type/id form.

-i

> Read a completed form from STDIN before submitting. This enables you to provide the manipulated input from a script or prepared form. The -o option is one way to generate a prepared form.

-o

> Dump the completed form to STDOUT instead of submitting. This provides a filled out form that you can copy and/or modify before returning it to *rt*. The -i option is one way to enter the contents of a dumped form.

-e

> Open the form in the editor even if the command line has enough information to make a submission directly. This overrides the default behavior.

-S *var=val*
> Submit the specified variable with the request.

There are three subactions for specifying values for each object. Each set, add, or del specification must be a distinct argument, but a subaction can have as many *field=value* pairs as you want.

set
> Sets the named field to the given value.

add
> Adds a value to a multi-valued field.

del
> Deletes the given value from the field.

Certain object types also allow attributes to be modified or deleted. If you try to modify an immutable field, (for example, created), *rt* will return an appropriate message indicating the error.

list

rt list [*options*] "*query string*"

The list action displays a list of objects selected by a TicketSQL query string. The query string is a required argument.

The ls and search actions are interchangable names for list. Use whatever suits your particular environment or taste.

The list action takes several options:

-i

> Return only the object type and numeric ID in the format type/id. This can be useful for feeding into a |rt edit - ... pipe.

-s

> Return a short object description.

-l

> Return a more detailed object description.

-t *type*

> Specifies one of the valid RT object types: ticket, user, group, queue.

-o +/-*field*

> Orders the returned list by the specified field. + for ascending order, - for descending order.

-S *var=val*

> Submits the specified variable with the request.

At the time of writing, list only works with ticket objects, although this may change soon to support all available RT types.

show

rt show [options] <object-ids>

The show action displays one or more objects identified by a unique alphanumeric object id. When referring to an RT object, remember that tickets only have numeric IDs, while users, groups, and queues have both numeric and alphanumeric identifiers that you can use interchangeably.

The show action has several options that may be used to improve the display of the requested object, depending on the relevance of each field in the current circumstances.

-

> Read object IDs from STDIN instead of the command line. Note that this is not simply the id but the combination of object type and the object id, or ids:
>
> > ticket/42
>
> or
>
> > ticket/1,12-33,42...

-t *type*

> Specifies one of the valid RT object types: ticket, user, group, queue.

-f *a,b,c*

> Restrict the display to the specified fields. These fields are *not* case-sensitive, but they need to be explicitly named in full, or RT will return empty fields in their place.

-S *var=val*

> Submits the specified variable with the request.

Although supplying an object type is required, RT will accept the type in the type/id form with multiple IDs separated by commas:

```
ticket/12,24,72
```

or in the -t *type id* form with multiple IDs separated by whitespace:

```
-t ticket 12 24 72
```

To give a range of IDs, use a - (dash) to separate the minimum and maximum numeric ID values:

```
ticket/12,24-30,72
-t ticket 12 24-30 72
```

Configuration

In order to connect to the RT server, rt needs a few pieces of information. The essential information rt requires is a server to connect to and access information for that server, but several other nonessential variables also are useful to know. Table C-1 lists the available configuration options.

Table C-1. Command-line configuration options

Option	Required	Description
Server name	yes	Specify which RT server to access. This should be a valid hostname. (If you can successfully ping the server using this name, everything should work as expected.)
User	yes	A valid username with access to the server defined.
Password	yes	The appropriate password for the username defined.
Order by	no	How to arrange the results of the query for actions that produce results.
Query string	no	A default query to use when an action requires a query but one isn't specified.
Debug level	no	A numeric value from 1 to 3 specifying how much *rt* should log. This is useful for debugging error messages or spurious failures. In normal usage this would not be set and would default to the value 0.
Configuration file	no	Tells *rt* to use a specific configuration file rather than search for the default *.rtrc*.
Text editor	no	Sets which editor to use when working from the command line. Defaults to vi if this variable is not set.

You can provide the above information to rt using environment variables or a configuration file, typically *.rtrc*. The configuration file can't define the location of the configuration file (for obvious reasons) or the debug level.

Environment Variables

The environment variables unique to rt are all prefixed by RT so as not to interfere with other applications. They are all Uppercase. The following is a list of all the supported variables.

```
RTUSER
RTPASSWD
RTSERVER
RTDEBUG
RTQUERY
RTORDERBY
RTCONFIG
EDITOR or VISUAL
```

The following example sets the essential variables in the *bash* shell:

```
$ export RTUSER=rtuser
$ export RTPASSWD=secret
$ export RTSERVER=rt.example.com
```

RTQUERY specifies a default query string:

```
$ export RTQUERY="Status='new' and Priority > 7"
```

With a default query in place, you can call show without any arguments, and it will use the default query:

```
$ rt show
```

You also might change the target server on-the-fly and request a particular ticket instead of using the default query specified in the environment:

```
$ RTSERVER=support.example.com rt show ticket/66
```

Or you might decide to put all this information in a custom configuration file (see "Configuration Files" later in this chapter). The RTCONFIG environment variable defines which configuration file to use:

```
$ export RTCONFIG=/rt/prod/config_file
```

RTCONFIG is useful when you have multiple different RT servers, perhaps one for internal use and one for external or client use. In this case you might create different configuration files to specify the RT server to access, appropriate user/password combinations and perhaps a default query string and switch between them on the fly:

```
$ RTCONFIG=./internal_rtrc rt show
...

$ RTCONFIG=./external_rtrc rt show
...
```

Setting environment variables on your operating system may have limitations or restrictions. See your OS and shell documentation for instructions on the various methods you can use to set them.

Note also that values set in environment variables override values set in the configuration file described below.

Configuration Files

Setting the environment variables for every shell can be troublesome, so *rt* provides a simpler way: configuration files. These configuration files are simple and consist of a small set of keywords and their values:

```
server https://rt.example.com
user jdoe
```

The keys for the configuration file are similar to the environment variables, but they don't have the RT prefix and they're all lowercase. The configuration file doesn't have keys equivalent to the RTDEBUG or RTCONFIG environment variables. The available settings are as follows:

```
server URL
user username
passwd password
query querystring
orderby order
```

If the environment variable RTCONFIG is not set, *rt* first looks for a configuration file with the name *.rtrc* in the current directory. If that file doesn't exist, *rt* searches for *.rtrc* in all parent directories up to the root directory, then in the user's home directory, and finally looks at */etc/rt.conf*. If *rt* is still missing the required server, user, and password information after searching for configuration files and inspecting the environment variables, it considers it a fatal error and forcibly quits.

The following example is a complete *rt* configuration file. Note that lines prefixed with the pound # sign are ignored, as are blank lines.

```
# This is a sample configuration file
user       rtuser
server     http://support.example.com
passwd     secret
query      "Status = 'new' and Priority > 5"
```

At this point, using either the environment variables, the configuration file method, or some combination of both, you should be able to setup *rt* to access any functional RT server at your disposal.

APPENDIX D
Required Perl Module Dependencies

This is a list of modules and minimum versions (where applicable) required for RT's installation. All of these modules are available on CPAN, *http://cpan.perl.org*.

This list is accurate as of RT 3.4.2. Newer versions of RT may require newer versions of modules.

Core

Cache::Simple::TimedExpiry
Class::ReturnValue (0.40)
DBI (1.37)
DBIx::SearchBuilder (1.26)
Digest::MD5 (2.27)
File::Spec (0.8)
File::Temp
HTML::Entities
Locale::Maketext (1.06)
Locale::Maketext::Fuzzy
Locale::Maketext::Lexicon (0.32)
Log::Dispatch (2.0)
MIME::Entity (5.108)
Mail::Mailer (1.57)
Module::Versions::Report
Net::Domain
Net::SMTP
Scalar::Util
Term::ReadKey
Test::Inline
Text::Autoformat
Text::Quoted (1.3)
Text::Template
Text::Wrapper

Time::ParseDate
Tree::Simple (1.0.4)
XMl::Simple

Mason
Apache::Session (1.53)
CGI (2.92)
CGI::Cookie (1.20)
Cache::Cache
Digest::MD5 (2.27)
Errno
Exception::Class (1.14)
FreezeThaw
HTML::Mason (1.23)
HTML::Server::Simple (0.07)
HTML::Server::Simple::Mason (0.03)
MLDBM
Params::Validate (0.02)
Storable (2.08)
XML::RSS

Mail gateway / CLI
Getopt::Long (2.24)
HTML::FormatText
HTML::TreeBuilder
LWP::UserAgent

FastCGI
FCGI
CGI::Fast

mod_perl 1.x
Apache::Request
Apache::DBI (0.92)

mod_perl 2.x
CGI (2.92)
Apache::DBI

Database (only the appropriate DBD module for your database is necessary)
DBD::mysql (2.1018)
DBD::Oracle
DBD::Pg
DBD::SQLite

Development Support
Apache::Test
HTML::Form

HTML::TokeParser
Module::Refresh (0.03)
Regexp::Common
Test::Inline
Test::WWW::Mechanize
WWW::Mechanize

Configuration File Reference

All of the configuration directives you can use in your *etc/RT_SiteConfig.pm* file are listed in this appendix.

Remember, never edit *RT_Config.pm*. Instead, add to *RT_SiteConfig.pm* and edit there.

Base Configuration

$rtname

$rtname is the string that RT looks for in-mail messages to figure out to which ticket a new piece of mail belongs.

Your domain name is recommended, so as not to pollute the namespace. Once you start using a given tag, you should probably never change it—otherwise, mail for existing tickets won't get put in the right place.

    Set($rtname, "example.com");

$EmailSubjectTagRegex

This regexp controls what subject tags RT recognizes as its own. Be very careful with it. Note that it overrides $rtname.

If you're not dealing with historical $rtname values, you'll likely never have to enable this feature:

    Set($EmailSubjectTagRegex, qr/\Q$rtname\E/);

$Organization

You should set this to your organization's DNS domain, for example, *fsck.com* or *asylum.arkham.ma.us*. The linking interface uses it to guarantee that ticket URIs are unique and easy to construct.

    Set($Organization, "example.com");

$MinimumPasswordLength

$MinimumPasswordLength defines the minimum length for user passwords. Setting it to 0 disables this check.

    Set($MinimumPasswordLength, "5");

`$Timezone`

> `$Timezone` is used to convert times entered by users into GMT and back again. It should be set to standard Unix timezone.
>
>   Set($Timezone, 'US/Eastern');

Database Configuration

`$DatabaseType`

> Database driver currently used. The value is case sensitive. Valid types are `mysql`, `Oracle`, and `Pg`.
>
>   Set($DatabaseType, 'mysql');

`$DatabaseHost`

> The domain name of your database server. If you're running MySQL and it's on *localhost*, leave it blank for enhanced performance.
>
>   Set($DatabaseHost, 'localhost');

`$DatabasePort`

> The port on which your database server runs. RT ignores this value unless it's a positive integer. It's usually safe to leave this blank.
>
>   Set($DatabasePort, 3306);

`$DatabaseUser`

> The name of the database user (inside the database).
>
>   Set($DatabaseUser, 'rt_user');

`$DatabasePassword`

> Password the DatabaseUser should use to access the database.
>
>   Set($DatabasePassword, 'p@ssw0rd');

`$DatabaseName`

> The name of the RT's database on your database server.
>
>   Set($DatabaseName, 'rt3');

`$DatabaseRequiresSSL`

> If you're using Postgres and have compiled in SSL support, set DatabaseRequireSSL to 1 to turn on SSL communication.
>
>   Set($DatabaseRequireSSL, undef);

Incoming Mail Gateway Configuration

`$OwnerEmail`

> OwnerEmail is the address of a human who manages RT. RT sends errors generated by the mail gateway to this address. This address should not be an address that's managed by your RT instance.
>
>   Set($OwnerEmail, 'root');

$LoopsToRTOwner

If $LoopsToRTOwner is defined, RT sends mail that it believes might be a loop to $RT::OwnerEmail.

    Set($LoopsToRTOwner, 1);

$StoreLoops

If $StoreLoops is defined, RT records messages that it believes to be part of mail loops. As it does this, it tries to be careful not to send mail to the sender of these messages.

    Set($StoreLoops, undef);

$MaxAttachmentSize

$MaxAttachmentSize sets the maximum size (in bytes) of attachments stored in the database.

For MySQL and Oracle, we set this size at 10 megabytes. If you're running a Postgres version earlier than 7.1, you need to drop this to 8192. (8k)

    Set($MaxAttachmentSize, 10000000);

$TruncateLongAttachments

$TruncateLongAttachments: if this is set to a non-undef value, RT truncates attachments longer than MaxAttachmentSize.

    Set($TruncateLongAttachments, undef);

$DropLongAttachments

$DropLongAttachments: if this is set to a non-undef value, RT silently drops attachments longer than MaxAttachmentSize.

    Set($DropLongAttachments, undef);

$ParseNewMessageForTicketCCs

If $ParseNewMessageForTicketCcs is true, RT attempts to divine ticket Cc watchers from the To and Cc lines of incoming messages. Be forewarned that if you have any addresses that forward mail to RT automatically, and you enable this option without modifying RTAddressRegexp below, you will get yourself into a heap of trouble.

    Set($ParseNewMessageForTicketCcs, undef);

$RTAddressRegexp

$RTAddressRegexp makes sure RT doesn't add itself as a ticket Cc if the setting above is enabled.

    Set($RTAddressRegexp, '^rt\@example.com$');

$CanonicalizeEmailAddressMatch *and* **$CanonicalizeEmailAddressReplace**

RT provides functionality that allows the system to rewrite incoming email addresses. In its simplest form, you can substitute the value in $CanonicalizeEmailAddressReplace for whatever the value is in $CanonicalizeEmailAddressMatch. These values are passed to the CanonicalizeEmailAddress subroutine in *RT/User.pm*. By default, that routine performs a s/*Match*/*Replace*/gi on any address passed to it.

```
Set($CanonicalizeEmailAddressMatch, '@subdomain\.example\.com$');
Set($CanonicalizeEmailAddressReplace, '@example.com');
```

$CanonicalizeOnCreate

If this is true, the page to create a new user passes the values that you enter in the form through the CanonicalizeUserInfo function in *User_Local.pm*.

```
Set($CanonicalizeOnCreate, 0);
```

$SenderMustExistInExternalDatabase

If you are using the LookupSenderInExternalDatabase option, and $SenderMustExistInExternalDatabase is true, RT refuses to create non-privileged accounts for unknown users. Instead, RT mails an error message and forwards the message to $RTOwner.

If you are not using $LookupSenderInExternalDatabase, this option has no effect.

If you define an AutoRejectRequest template, RT uses this template for the rejection message.

```
Set($SenderMustExistInExternalDatabase, undef);
```

Outgoing Mail Configuration

$CorrespondAddress *and* $CommentAddress

RT is designed so that any mail that already has a ticket ID associated with it gets to the right place automatically.

$CorrespondAddress and $CommentAddress are the default addresses for From: and Reply-To: headers of correspondence and comment mail tracked by RT, unless overridden by a queue-specific address.

```
Set($CorrespondAddress, 'correspond@rt.example.com');

Set($CommentAddress, 'comment@rt.example.com');
```

$MailCommand

$MailCommand defines which method RT uses to try to send mail. We know that *sendmailpipe* works fairly well. If *sendmailpipe* doesn't work well for you, try *sendmail*.

Note that you should remove the -t from $SendmailArguments if you use *sendmail* rather than *sendmailpipe*.

```
Set($MailCommand, 'sendmailpipe');
```

$SendmailArguments

$SendmailArguments defines what flags to pass to $Sendmail assuming you picked *sendmail* or *sendmailpipe* as the $MailCommand above. If you picked *sendmailpipe*, you must add a -t flag to $SendmailArguments.

These options are good for most Sendmail wrappers and workalikes:

```
Set($SendmailArguments, "-oi -t");
```

These arguments are good for Sendmail 8 and newer:

```
Set($SendmailArguments,"-oi -t -ODeliveryMode=b -OErrorMode=m");
```

$SendmailPath

If you selected this *sendmailpipe*, you must specify the path to your Sendmail binary in $SendmailPath. If you did not select this *sendmailpipe*, this has no effect.

```
Set($SendmailPath, "/usr/sbin/sendmail");
```

$UseFriendlyFromLine

By default, RT sets the outgoing mail's From: header to *SenderName* via RT. Setting this option to 0 disables it.

```
Set($UseFriendlyFromLine, 1);
```

$FriendlyFromLineFormat

The sprintf() format of the friendly From: header; its arguments are Sender-Name and SenderEmailAddress.

```
Set($FriendlyFromLineFormat, "\"%s via RT\" <%s>");
```

$UseFriendlyToLine

RT can set an optional friendly To: header when sending messages to Ccs or AdminCcs rather than having a blank To: header.

This feature does not work with Sendmail. If you are using Sendmail, rather than Postfix, qmail, Exim, or some other MTA, you must disable this option.

```
Set($UseFriendlyToLine, 0);
```

$FriendlyToLineFormat

sprintf() format of the friendly From: header; its arguments are WatcherType and TicketId.

```
Set($FriendlyToLineFormat, "\"%s of $RT::rtname Ticket #%s\":;");
```

$NotifyActor

By default, RT doesn't notify the person who performs an update, as they already know what they've done. If you'd like to change this behavior, set $NotifyActor to 1.

```
Set($NotifyActor, 0);
```

$RecordOutgoingEmail

By default, RT records each message it sends out to its own internal database. To change this behavior, set $RecordOutgoingEmail to 0.

```
Set($RecordOutgoingEmail, 1);
```

Logging

The default configuration logs anything except debugging information to syslog. See the Log::Dispatch documentation for more information about alternate delivery mechanisms.

It may make sense to send error and higher by email to some administrator. If you do this, be careful that this email isn't sent to back to the current RT instance.

$LogToSyslog, $LogToScree, *and* $LogToFile

These options define minimum log level that each output mechanism logs. From lowest level to highest, the choices are:

```
debug
info
notice
warning
error
critical
alert
emergency
```

For historical reasons, you must use '' (empty string) instead of 0 or undef when disabling a logging mechanism.

```
Set($LogToSyslog    , 'debug');
Set($LogToScreen    , 'error');
Set($LogToFile      , '');
Set($LogDir, '/home/rspier/projects/rt-3.4/var/log');
Set($LogToFileNamed , "rt.log");
```

@LogToSyslogConf

If you are using Syslog logging, this directive allows you to override any other options RT passes to Log::Dispatch::Syslog. See the Log::Dispatch::Syslog documentation for more information about interesting flags, including facility, logopt, and ident.

On systems such as Solaris or UnixWare that don't provide a UNIX domain socket to syslog, set this (socket => 'inet').

```
@LogToSyslogConf = () unless (@LogToSyslogConf);
```

Web Interface Configuration

$WebPath

This defines the directory name to be used for images in RT web documents.

If you've configured your webserver to have the path to RT somewhere other than at the root of your server, $WebPath requires a leading / (slash) but no trailing /.

```
Set($WebPath, "");
```

$WebBaseURL

This is the scheme, server, and port for constructing URLs to RT. $WebBaseURL doesn't need a trailing /.

```
Set($WebBaseURL, "http://RT::WebBaseURL.not.configured:80");
```

$WebImagesURL

$WebImagesURL points to the base URL where RT can find its images.

```
Set($WebImagesURL, $WebPath . "/NoAuth/images/");
```

$LogoURL

$LogoURL points to the URL of the RT logo displayed in the web interface.

```
Set($LogoURL, $WebImagesURL . "bplogo.gif");
```

$WebNoAuthRegex

$WebNoAuthRegex matches the portion of RT's URL space that should not require authentication.

```
Set($WebNoAuthRegex, qr!^(?:/+NoAuth/|
                         /+REST/\d+\.\d+/NoAuth/)!x );
```

$MessageBoxWidth

For message boxes, set the entry box width and what type of wrapping to use. Defaults to 72.

```
Set($MessageBoxWidth, 72);
```

$MessageBoxWrap

Choose between HARD wrapping and SOFT wrapping. The default is HARD.

```
Set($MessageBoxWrap, "HARD");
```

$TrustHTMLAttachments

If $TrustHTMLAttachments is not defined, RT displays attachments as text. This prevents malicious HTML and Javascript from being sent in a request (although there is more to it than that).

```
Set($TrustHTMLAttachments, undef);
```

$RedistributeAutoGeneratedMessages

A true value (the default) tells RT to redistribute correspondence that it identifies as machine generated. Setting this to 0 tells RT not to redistribute such messages. You also can set it to privileged, which redistributes only to privileged users. This is useful if you get malformed bounces caused by autocreated requestors with bogus addresses.

```
Set($RedistributeAutoGeneratedMessages, 1);
```

$PreferRichText

If $PreferRichText is set to a true value, RT shows HTML/rich text messages in preference to their plain text alternatives. RT scrubs the HTML to show only a minimal subset of HTML to avoid possible contamination by cross-site scripting attacks.

```
Set($PreferRichText, undef);
```

$WebExternalAuth

If $WebExternalAuth is defined, RT defers to the environment's REMOTE_USER variable.

```
Set($WebExternalAuth, undef);
```

$WebFallbackToInternalAuth

If `$WebFallbackToInternalAuth` is undefined, the user is allowed a chance of fall-back to the login screen, even if `REMOTE_USER` failed.

```
Set($WebFallbackToInternalAuth, undef);
```

$WebExternalGecos

`$WebExternalGecos` means to match the gecos field as the user identity; useful with *mod_auth_pwcheck* and IIS Integrated Windows logon.

```
Set($WebExternalGecos, undef);
```

$WebExternalAuto

`$WebExternalAuto` creates users under the same name as `REMOTE_USER` upon login, if it's missing in the Users table.

```
Set($WebExternalAuto, undef);
```

$WebSessionClass

`$WebSessionClass` is the class you wish to use for managing sessions. It defaults to use your SQL database, but if you are using MySQL 3.x and plan to use non-ASCII queue names, add the following line to *RT_SiteConfig.pm* to prevent session corruption.

```
Set($WebSessionClass, 'Apache::Session::File');
```

$WebFlushDbCacheEveryRequest

By default, RT clears its database cache after every page view. This ensures that you've always got the most current information when working in a multi-process environment (mod_perl or FastCGI). Setting `$WebFlushDbCacheEveryRequest` to 0 turns this off, which speeds RT up a bit, at the expense of some data accuracy.

```
Set($WebFlushDbCacheEveryRequest, '1');
```

$MaxInlineBody

`$MaxInlineBody` is the maximum attachment size that RT uses to display inline when viewing a transaction. 13456 is a semi-random but sane default.

```
Set($MaxInlineBody, 13456);
```

$MyTicketsLength

`$MyTicketsLength` is the length of the owned tickets table on the front page. For some people, the default of 10 isn't big enough to get a feel for how much work needs to be done before you get some time off.

```
Set($MyTicketsLength, 10);
```

$MyRequestsLength

`$MyRequestsLength` is the length of the requested tickets table on the front page.

```
Set($MyRequestsLength, 10);
```

@MasonParameters

`@MasonParameters` is a list of parameters for the constructor of HTML::Mason's Apache or CGI Handler. This is normally only useful for debugging, for example, profiling individual components with:

```
    use MasonX::Profiler; # available on CPAN
    @MasonParameters = (preamble => 'my $p = MasonX::Profiler->new($m, $r);');

    @MasonParameters = () unless (@MasonParameters);
```

$DefaultSearchResultFormat

> $DefaultSearchResultFormat is the default format for RT search results:

```
    Set ($DefaultSearchResultFormat, qq{
      '<B><A HREF="$RT::WebPath/Ticket/Display.html?id=__id__">__id__</a></B>/TITLE:
    #',
      '<B><A HREF="$RT::WebPath/Ticket/Display.html?id=__id__">__Subject__</a></B>/
    TITLE:Subject',
      Status,
      QueueName,
      OwnerName,
      Priority,
      '__NEWLINE__',
      '',
      '<small>__Requestors__</small>',
      '<small>__CreatedRelative__</small>',
      '<small>__ToldRelative__</small>',
      '<small>__LastUpdatedRelative__</small>',
      '<small>__TimeLeft__</small>'});
```

RT UTF-8 Settings

@LexiconLanguages

> @LexiconLanguages is an array that contains languages supported by RT's inter-
> nationalization interface. It defaults to all supplied translations. Setting it to a
> shorter list, such as qw(en ja), makes RT bilingual instead of multilingual, but it
> saves some memory.

```
    @LexiconLanguages = qw(*) unless (@LexiconLanguages);
```

@EmailInputEncodings

> @EmailInputEncodings is an array that contains default encodings used to guess
> which charset an attachment uses if not specified. These encodings must be rec-
> ognized by Encode::Guess.

```
    @EmailInputEncodings = qw(utf-8 iso-8859-1 us-ascii) unless
    (@EmailInputEncodings);
```

$EmailOutputEncoding

> $EmailOutputEncoding is the character set for outbound email. Its value must be
> recognized by Encode.

```
    Set($EmailOutputEncoding , 'utf-8');
```

RT Date Handling Options (for Time::ParseDate)

$DateDayBeforeMonth

Set $DateDayBeforeMonth to 1 if your local date convention looks like *dd/mm/yy* instead of *mm/dd/yy*.

    Set($DateDayBeforeMonth , 1);

$AmbiguousDayInPast

Should "Tuesday" default to meaning "Next Tuesday" or "Last Tuesday"?

Set to 0 for "Next" or 1 for "Last."

    Set($AmbiguousDayInPast , 1);

Miscellaneous RT Settings

@ActiveStatus *and* @InactiveStatus

You can define new statuses and even reorder existing statuses here. Warning: do not delete any of the default statuses. If you do, RT breaks horribly.

    @ActiveStatus = qw(new open stalled) unless @ActiveStatus;
    @InactiveStatus = qw(resolved rejected deleted) unless @InactiveStatus;

$Devel Mode

RT comes with a development mode setting. As a convenience for developers, this setting turns on all sorts of development options that you most likely don't want in production.

It turns off Mason's static_source directive. By default, you can't edit RT's web interface components on the fly and have RT pick up your changes.

    Set($DevelMode, '0');

Index

We'd like to hear your suggestions for improving our indexes. Send email to *index@oreilly.com*.

About the Authors

Jesse Vincent first wrote RT during a summer internship at a web development shop after his sophomore year at Wesleyan University. After graduation, he spent a year in Seattle working on instant messaging for Microsoft. A year later, he came back to the world of Unix and open source as the systems lead at a now defunct dotcom, only to find people actively using RT—motivated by guilt, he rewrote it from scratch. 18 months later, he realized he was spending more time on his hobby (RT) than his day job, and founded Best Practical Solutions, a company dedicated to maintaining and supporting RT and other tools to help people get work done. When he's not working on RT, Jesse spends his time working on RT.

Robert Spier first came upon RT in late 1997, and has been working with it ever since. He rewrote the search infrastructure for RT 3.0 because he had itches that begged to be scratched. He currently manages a software development team at a post-boom Internet company. In his spare time, he teaches RT Developer Training courses and maintains the perl.org infrastructure—including perlbug: the Perl bug tracking system. When not sitting in front of a computer, he volunteers at a local animal rescue.

Dave Rolsky is a programmer, author, and activist with a background in music composition, and various geeky interests, including the works of Gene Wolfe, films, and the workings of time zones. He has been actively developing Free Software (Perl) for several years and is a member of the Mason core development team.

Darren Chamberlain is a system administrator and recovering programmer living and working in the Boston area.

Richard Foley is a Munich-based Perl and Oracle developer who spends most of his time allegedly programming, when he could be spending quality time with his family, walking, or skiing in the nearby Alps. He has a background in technical illustration and has developed software applications for the aerospace, Internet, and banking industries.

Colophon

Our look is the result of reader comments, our own experimentation, and feedback from distribution channels. Distinctive covers complement our distinctive approach to technical topics, breathing personality and life into potentially dry subjects.

The animal on the cover of *RT Essentials* is a northern harrier (*Circus cyaneus*). Harrier is the common name for 13 species of birds of prey, characterized by long legs, long, broad wings, and an owl-like ruffle of feathers surrounding the face.

Long known as the marsh hawk in the United States and as the hen harrier in England, the northern harrier is the only species of harrier found in North America.

A full-grown adult will normally be between 16 and 24 inches in length. The females often grow to be larger than the males.

Northern harriers inhabit open country, primarily marshes and grasslands. They hunt by crisscrossing the area at a low elevation, then dropping on their prey. They feed on small rodents, frogs, snakes, and occasionally birds. In search of prey, the harrier will cover up to 100 miles per day, detecting small animals with its extremely keen hearing.

The northern harrier is considered one of the most agile and acrobatic birds in North America. During the breeding season, the male performs a spectacular courtship flight consisting of a series of U-shaped maneuvers.

Darren Kelly was the production editor, and Julie Campbell was the copyeditor and proofreader for *RT Essentials*. Jamie Peppard and Colleen Gorman provided quality control. Julie Bess wrote the index. Amy Hassos provided production services.

Ellie Volckhausen designed the cover of this book, based on a series design by Edie Freedman. The cover image is a 19th-century engraving from the Dover Pictorial Archive. Karen Montgomery produced the cover layout with Adobe InDesign CS using Adobe's ITC Garamond font.

David Futato designed the interior layout. This book was converted by Keith Fahlgren to FrameMaker 5.5.6 with a format conversion tool created by Erik Ray, Jason McIntosh, Neil Walls, and Mike Sierra that uses Perl and XML technologies. The text font is Linotype Birka; the heading font is Adobe Myriad Condensed; and the code font is LucasFont's TheSans Mono Condensed. The illustrations that appear in the book were produced by Robert Romano, Jessamyn Read, and Lesley Borash using Macromedia FreeHand MX and Adobe Photoshop CS. The tip and warning icons were drawn by Christopher Bing. This colophon was written by Darren Kelly.

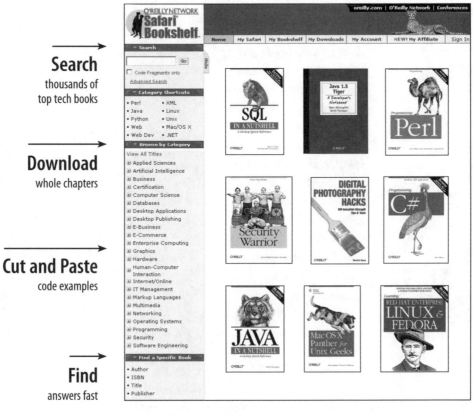

Related Titles from O'Reilly

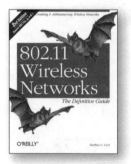

Networking

802.11 Security

802.11 Wireless Networks: The Definitive Guide, *2nd Edition*

Asterisk: The Future of Telephony

BGP

Building Wireless Community Networks, *2nd Edition*

Cisco Cookbook

Cisco IOS Access Lists

Cisco IOS in a Nutshell, *2nd Edition*

DNS & BIND Cookbook

DNS & BIND, 4th Edition

Essential SNMP, *2nd Edition*

IP Routing

IPv6 Essentials

IPv6 Network Administration

LDAP System Administration

Managing NFS and NIS, *2nd Edition*

Network Troubleshooting Tools

RADIUS

sendmail 8.13 Companion

sendmail, *3rd Edition*

sendmail Cookbook

SpamAssassin

Switching to VOIP

TCP/IP Network Administration, *3rd Edition*

Unix Backup and Recovery

Using Samba, *2nd Edition*

Using SANs and NAS

Windows Server 2003 Network Administration

O'REILLY®

Our books are available at most retail and online bookstores.

To order direct: 1-800-998-9938 • *order@oreilly.com* • *www.oreilly.com*

Online editions of most O'Reilly titles are available by subscription at *safari.oreilly.com*

Keep in touch with O'Reilly

Download examples from our books

To find example files from a book, go to:
www.oreilly.com/catalog select the book,
and follow the "Examples" link.

Register your O'Reilly books

Register your book at *register.oreilly.com*
Why register your books? Once you've
registered your O'Reilly books you can:

- Win O'Reilly books, T-shirts or discount
  coupons in our monthly drawing.
- Get special offers available only to
  registered O'Reilly customers.
- Get catalogs announcing new books
  (US and UK only).
- Get email notification of new editions
  of the O'Reilly books you own.

Join our email lists

Sign up to get topic-specific email announ-
cements of new books and conferences,
special offers, and O'Reilly Network
technology newsletters at:

elists.oreilly.com

It's easy to customize your free elists subscription so you'll get exactly the O'Reilly news
you want.

Get the latest news, tips, and tools

www.oreilly.com

- "Top 100 Sites on the Web"—PC Magazine
- CIO Magazine's Web Business 50 Awards

Our web site contains a library of comprehensive product information (including book
excerpts and tables of contents), downloadable
software, background articles, interviews with
technology leaders, links to relevant sites, book
cover art, and more.

Work for O'Reilly

Check out our web site for current
employment opportunities:

jobs.oreilly.com

Contact us

O'Reilly Media, Inc.
1005 Gravenstein Hwy North
Sebastopol, CA 95472 USA
Tel: 707-827-7000 or 800-998-9938
    (6am to 5pm PST)
Fax: 707-829-0104

Contact us by email

For answers to problems regarding
your order or our products:
order@oreilly.com

To request a copy of our latest catalog:
catalog@oreilly.com

For book content technical questions
or corrections: **booktech@oreilly.com**

For educational, library, government,
and corporate sales: **corporate@oreilly.com**

To submit new book proposals to our
editors and product managers:
proposals@oreilly.com

For information about our international
distributors or translation queries:
international@oreilly.com

For information about academic
use of O'Reilly books:
adoption@oreilly.com
or visit:
academic.oreilly.com

For a list of our distributors outside
of North America check out:
international.oreilly.com/distributors.html

Order a book online

www.oreilly.com/order_new